ADVENTIST PIONEER LIBRARY

The Prophetic Gift

IN THE
GOSPEL CHURCH

J. N. LOUGHBOROUGH

© 2022 ADVENTIST PIONEER LIBRARY
P. O. Box 51264
Eugene, OR, 97405
www.APLib.org

Originally published in 1911 by the *Pacific Press Publishing Association*

Published in the USA

November, 2022

ISBN: 978-1-61455-123-2

The original page numbers of the 1911 printed edition of this book are found within brackets throughout the text.

ADVENTIST PIONEER LIBRARY

The Prophetic Gift

IN THE
GOSPEL CHURCH

"SO THAT YE COME BEHIND IN NO GIFT; WAITING
FOR THE COMING OF OUR LORD JESUS CHRIST."
1 CORINTHIANS 1:7.

J. N. LOUGHBOROUGH

JOHN NORTON LOUGHBOROUGH
1832-1924

CONTENTS

Foreword 7
Preface 9
Part 1 11
    Angelic Instruction 11
    Ancient Prophets 12
    Women as Prophets 14
    The Son Speaking 15
    Prophecy of Joel 16
    Promise of the Spirit 17
    The Temple of the Spirit 18
    Manifestation of the Spirit 19
    Charity, or Love 20
    Prophecy in the Early Church 20
    The Apostasy 21
    The Refreshing 23
    Perilous Times 24
    Final Deliverance 24
    Law and Prophet's Message 25
    Spirit of Prophecy 25
    Prophesyings 26
    Proving the Gift 27
    Conclusion 28

Part 2 29
    Practical Working of the Gift 38
    Comparison 40
    Another Comparison 41
    Angelic Influence Illustrated 42
    Satan's Plans Defeated 43
    Dorchester Vision 44
    Prophetic Delineation of Character 45
    Developments at Vergennes, Michigan 47
    Rules for Discerning True Prophets 49
    Rule One 50
    Rule Two — True Prophets 50

Rule Three — False Prophets	51
Rule Four	51
True and False Prophets Compared	52
Rule Five — True Prophecies are Fulfilled	53
True Prophecies	56
Vision of the Civil War	57
Messenger Party	60
"Be in Health"	61
Otsego Vision	62
Predictions Concerning Sunday Laws	63
Catholic and Protestant Unity	64
Catholic and Methodist St. Patrick's Day	65
Prediction of Sanitarium Sites	66
Rule Six — Miracles Not a Test of a True Prophet	67
Rule Seven — "By Their Fruits Ye Shall Know Them"	69

Foreword

John Norton Loughborough (1832-1924) was converted to Seventh-day Adventism at the age of twenty. (1852) He immediately went forth to proclaim the third angel's message, supporting himself by carpentry since there was no organized work at that time.

He was ordained in 1854 and worked in New York, Pennsylvania and the Middle West. In 1868 he and D. T. Bourdeau went to California to pioneer the work there. By 1871 he had helped to establish five churches. In 1878 he baptized the first three members in Nevada. Then went on to England to pioneer the work there.

Through the years he held such positions as Conference President, General Conference Treasurer and evangelist.

He wrote several books which are all still in demand by scholars.

His final active work (except for occasional speaking engagements at some of the camp meetings) was to tour the world in 1908 visiting SDA establishments in Europe, Australia, Africa and New Zealand.

Preface

READING in the Old Testament Scriptures how frequently the Lord spoke to His people through prophets, by whom He "multiplied" visions; and the record in the New Testament that "when He [Christ] ascended up on high" He placed the prophetic gift "in the church" (Ephesians 4:8-11), leads many to inquire: "Why is not the gift of prophecy still manifested among the Lord's people? Can it be that the end of all things is to come, and the Lord not speak directly to His children to prepare them for that event?" The following pages present an answer to the above questions.

In Part One of this book it is shown how God spoke to His people in ancient times, and also in apostolic times, and how, as the result of apostasy in the church, there has been a lack of the manifestations of His Spirit. Here, also, is considered *what* the Lord has promised to do in the *"refreshing"* that is to precede His coming.

In Part Two is a consideration of facts respecting a manifestation of the gift of prophecy as connected with *"the great second advent movement."* For over fifty-eight years the writer has been acquainted with this gift, and its manifestation through Mrs. E. G. White. Having been privileged to see her in "open vision" nearly fifty times, he speaks of that which he has seen and knows. Since 1884 her visions have been about as frequent as formerly, [4] but instead of being "open visions," they are now what the Scriptures call "night visions," for a description of which see pages 7 and 8 of this book.

The Bible proofs and narrated facts in the following pages are submitted to the candid reader by one who believes fully that the Lord is again visiting His people through the gift of prophecy. May we all, in this study, follow the advice of the apostle Paul to "prove all things; hold fast that which is good." 1 Thessalonians 5:21.

J. N. LOUGHBOROUGH.
Lodi, California, March 1, 1911.

Part I

"GOD, who at sundry times and in divers manners spake in time past unto the fathers by the prophets, hath in these last days spoken unto us by His Son, whom He hath appointed heir of all things, by whom also He made the worlds." Hebrews 1:1, 2.

The above text clearly shows that the Lord has had various ways of speaking to His people in different periods of time. In the earliest record of the human race found in Biblical history, before sin entered the world, man had communion with God face to face. We learn also that after man had sinned the Lord instructed His people in an audible voice. In this manner He addressed Adam (Genesis 3:8-18); Cain (Genesis 4:6-15); Noah (Genesis 6:13-22; 7:1-5; 8:15; 9:8, 12, 17); Abraham (Genesis 17:1-6); Isaac (Genesis 26:2-5); Jacob (Genesis 28:13); Moses (Numbers 12:6-8); and Samuel (1 Samuel 3:4).

Angelic Instruction

The Lord spoke also to men through the agency of angels. These holy beings are not, as some suppose, the spirits of dead men, but are beings of a higher order than men, as man was made "a little lower than the angels." Hebrews 2:7. In those ancient times Satan transformed himself into an angel [6] of light, sought to lead men into a false worship of their dead friends and heroes, and represented himself and angels as being the spirits of their dead. The Lord plainly said of such worship and transactions that what was professedly offered to the dead was in reality sacrificed to devils-fallen angels. See Deuteronomy 32:17; Psalm 106:28, 35-37; 1 Corinthians 10:20. Under the Mosaic dispensation He strictly forbade any such "consulting with familiar spirits," specifying a death penalty for such an offense. Leviticus 17:7; 19:31; 20:27; Deuteronomy 18:10-13. The pure, holy angels are "sent forth to minister for them who shall be heirs of salvation" (Hebrews 1:7, 14); but they never come to represent dead persons.

Through the instrumentality of angels the Lord has often communicated His will to men. In this manner He spoke to Abraham (Genesis 18:1-3); to Lot (Genesis 19:1); to Joshua (Joshua 5:13-15); to Gideon (Judges 6:11-22); and to Manoah (Judges 13).

ANCIENT PROPHETS

Another mode of communication was by prophets, through visions and dreams. Of these the Lord said, "If there be a prophet among you, I the Lord will make Myself known unto him in a vision, and will speak unto him in a dream." Numbers 12:6.

Of the visions given to God's servants the prophets, there seem to have been two kinds—one called "open visions," or those given where the individual could be seen while in the vision, and the other called "night visions." Reference is made to the [7] former visions in 1 Samuel 3:1, where is found the experience of the child Samuel in these words: "The word of the Lord was precious in those days; there was no open vision." There were prophets in those days who had instructions from the Lord, but their visions were not given to them openly before the people. In the previous chapter, at the same date of Samuel's vision—1165 B.C.—there came "a man of God"—a prophet—to Eli, and told him of his wrongs, and predicted the fate of his two sons, that they should both die in one day, etc. 1 Samuel 2:27, 30, 33. In the same chapter where it is said, "There was no *open* vision," is the record of the vision given to Samuel. It was not an *open* vision. Not even did Eli see Samuel in the vision. The Lord taught him the tidings he was to bear to Eli. The record of the following morning says, "And Samuel feared to show Eli *the vision.*" 1 Samuel 3:15. Samuel at this time had a vision from God, although it was not an *open* vision. His vision then must have been of the same character as that called in other portions of the Scripture a

NIGHT VISION

"God spake unto Israel in the visions of the night." Genesis 46:2. The dream of Nebuchadnezzar was "revealed unto Daniel in a night vision." Daniel 2:19. So also Daniel himself had a view, "in the night visions," of Christ coming to the Father to receive His kingdom. Daniel 7:13. On another occasion he was taken in vision in the midst of Chaldeans. [8] Had they remained, they might have seen him in the vision (an open vision); but, instead, "a great quaking fell upon them, so that they fled to hide themselves." Daniel 10:7.

On turning to the New Testament we find that in Paul's experience a vision appeared to him in the night. Acts 16:9. And again it was in the night season that he received that valuable instruction in reference to the shipwreck at Melita. Acts 27:23, 24. He was also encouraged in a night vision at Corinth. Acts 18:9. So also in a night vision the Lord showed him that he must bear witness for Him in Rome. Acts 23:11. In Ezekiel 8:1-3 is a record of one of Ezekiel's visions, before the elders—an open vision. The vision of Cornelius (Acts 10:3, Revised Version) was "a vision openly." It occurred "the ninth hour"—"the hour of prayer" (Acts 3:1), when his family were assembled for prayer. From the above texts it will be observed that these night visions are treated in the Scriptures as of the same force and origin as the "open visions."

The following statement in reference to dreams and night visions is found in the book of Job: "For God speaketh once, yea twice, yet man perceiveth it not. In a dream, in a vision of the night, when deep sleep falleth upon men, in slumberings upon the bed; then He openeth the ears of men, and sealeth their instruction, that He may withdraw man from his purpose, and hide pride from man." Chapter 33:14-17. See also Job 4:13-17. [9]

This mode of communication by prophets was not a matter of rare occurrence in those olden times, for the Lord said of it, "I have also spoken by the prophets, and I have *multiplied* visions, and used similitudes, by the ministry of the prophets." Hosea 12:10. He thus testified to them "by all the prophets." 2 Kings 17:13. This He did "betimes" ("continually and carefully," margin). 2 Chronicles 36:15. Through these prophets He pleaded with the people to flee from idolatry, saying, "Oh, do not this abominable thing that I hate." Jeremiah 44:4. The masses, with their rulers, continued in their wickedness, "belied the Lord," and their prophets became wind. Jeremiah 5:12, 13. "They set up their ensigns for signs," and there was "no more any prophet." Psalm 74:4, 9. Then they sought "a vision" from the Lord, but they found none, because the law perished from the priest. Ezekiel 7:26. When the people were thus left without a prophet it was a source of great loss to them, as shown by the words of Azariah, the son of Oded, to Asa, king of Judah, when he said: "Now for a long season Israel hath been without the true God, and without a teaching priest, and without law. But when they in their trouble did turn unto the Lord God of Israel, and sought Him, He was found of them." 2 Chronicles 15:3, 4.

While Uzziah, king of Judah, gave heed to the word of the Lord by His prophets, prosperity attended him. The record says: "He sought God in [10] the days of Zechariah, who had understanding in the visions of God: and as long as he sought the Lord, God made him to prosper." "But when he was strong, his heart was lifted up to his destruction: for he transgressed against the Lord his God, and went into the temple of the Lord to burn incense." "And Uzziah the king was a leper unto the day of his death." 2 Chronicles 26:5, 16, 21.

Notwithstanding all these tokens of God's favor, this people fell again into idolatry, and the Lord testified to them by the prophet Jeremiah: "If ye will not harken to Me, to walk in My law, which I have set before you, to harken to the words of My servants the prophets, whom I sent unto you, both rising up early, and sending them, but ye have not harkened; then will I make this house like Shiloh, and will make this city a curse to all the nations of the earth." Jeremiah 26:4-6.

Disregarding the admonition of the Lord, the people were brought into a position at last where they could see the force of the words of Solomon, when he said, "Where there is no vision, the people perish [cast off restraint, R. V.]: but he that keepeth the law, happy is he." Proverbs 29:18. Still, however, they persisted in following their own way, walking in the imaginations of their own hearts, until their city was laid in ruins. Then came the lamentation of the prophet Jeremiah: "Her gates are sunk into the ground; ... the law is no more; her prophets also find no vision from the Lord." Lamentations 2:9. [11]

WOMEN AS PROPHETS

In Old Testament times the Lord not only used men as prophets, but also devout women were favored with this gift. In the days of the judges of

Israel we have the record of Deborah, the wife of Lapidoth, who was not only a prophetess, but served in the position of judge. Through instructions given by her, their enemies were overthrown, as seen in Judges 4:4; 5:31. Then again mention is made of Huldah the prophetess, the wife of Shallum the son of Tikvah, in the days of Josiah, the good king of Judah. She seems to have been connected with the school at Jerusalem, and was sought for counsel, as recorded in 2 Kings 22:13-20; 2 Chronicles 34:22-28.

At the time the Saviour was taken to the temple to have made for Him the required offering, the devoted Simeon recognized Him as the promised Messiah. And there was also present upon that occasion Anna, a *prophetess*, who dwelt in the temple-probably in the "college," or "school," as did Huldah. Thus it is evident that when Peter on the day of Pentecost—in harmony with Joel's prophecy—declared that as a result of the outpouring of the Spirit, the "handmaidens" and "daughters" should prophesy, it was not a strange thing to the church to learn that women should share in the prophetic gift in the gospel age. [12]

THE SON SPEAKING

He who spoke in divers manners in old time, "hath in these last days spoken unto us by His Son." This of course includes Christ's personal teaching when on the earth, as we have it in the four Gospels of the New Testament. That was not, however, the whole of His teaching for the "last days;" for when He was about to leave the world, He said to His disciples, "I will pray the Father, and He shall give you another Comforter, that He may abide with you forever." John 14:16. Respecting this Comforter, He said, "But the Comforter, which is the Holy Ghost, whom the Father will send in My name, He shall teach you all things, and bring all things to your remembrance, whatsoever I have said unto you." John 14:26. Again, "But when the Comforter is come, whom I will send unto you from the Father, even the Spirit of truth, which proceedeth from the Father, He shall testify of Me." John 15:26.

Of the special work of the Comforter, which was to "abide forever," the Saviour said: "It is expedient for you that I go away: for if I go not away, the Comforter will not come unto you; but if I depart, I will send Him unto you. And when He is come, He will reprove the world of sin, and of righteousness, and of judgment: of sin, because they believe not on Me; of righteousness, because I go to My Father, and ye see Me no more; of judgment, because the prince of this world is judged. I have [13] yet many things to say unto you, but ye can not bear them now." John 16:7-12.

All that was to be spoken by the Son was not accomplished when He was here in person; for He said: "Howbeit when He, the Spirit of truth, is come, He will guide you into all truth; for He shall not speak of Himself; but whatsoever He shall hear, that shall He speak: and He will show you things to come. He shall glorify Me, for He shall receive of Mine, and shall show it unto you." John 16:13, 14. Of the coming and work of the Spirit, our Lord further spoke to the disciples: "And, behold, I send the promise of My Father upon you: but tarry ye in the city of Jerusalem, until ye be endued with power from on high." Luke 24:49. A record of the same conversation is also given in these words: "And, being assembled together with them, commanded them that they should not depart from Jerusalem, but wait for the promise [fulfillment of the promise] of the Father, which, saith He, ye have heard of Me. For John truly baptized with water; but ye shall be baptized with the Holy Ghost not many days hence." Acts 1:4, 5.

Prophecy of Joel

This promise which the Father had made, and to which our Saviour here refers, must be the promise recorded in the book of Joel; for when, on the day of Pentecost, the Spirit was poured out, Peter recognized it as the beginning of what was predicted by Joel. We read: "And when the day [14] of Pentecost was fully come, they were all with one accord in one place. And suddenly there came a sound from heaven as of a rushing mighty wind, and it filled all the house where they were sitting. And there appeared unto them cloven tongues like as of fire, and it sat upon each of them. And they were all filled with the Holy Ghost, and began to speak with other tongues, as the Spirit gave them utterance." Acts 2:1-4.

The mocking ones among the multitude who came together on seeing and hearing of this wonderful manifestation, said: "These men are full of new wine. But Peter, standing up with the eleven, lifted up his voice, and said unto them, Ye men of Judea, and all ye that dwell at Jerusalem, be this known unto you, and harken to my words; for these are not drunken, as ye suppose, seeing it is but the third hour of the day. [The force of Peter's plea is more fully realized when we consider that in all their feasts they were forbidden to drink anything but water, until the fourth hour.] But this is that which was spoken by the prophet Joel; And it shall come to pass in the last days, saith God, I will pour out of My Spirit upon all flesh; and your sons and your daughters shall prophesy, and your young men shall see visions, and your old men shall dream dreams; and on My servants and on My handmaidens I will pour out in those days of My Spirit; and they shall prophesy; and I will show wonders in heaven above, and signs [15] in the earth beneath; blood, and fire, and vapor of smoke; the sun shall be turned into darkness, and the moon into blood, before that great and notable day of the Lord come." Acts 2:13-20; Joel 2:28-32.

In Joel's prediction of what should result from the outpouring of the Spirit, nothing was said about tongues. This is, nevertheless, one of the operations of the Spirit of God, as well as those directly specified in Joel's prophecy, and all were to be seen in the work of the Spirit. The time covered by this prophecy of Joel reaches down to the close of probationary time—even to the "great and terrible day of the Lord." The "*last* days" must include the very last day of the last days, which would take in the last day of probationary time. Hence this prediction of Joel relates to the work of the Spirit of God—the Comforter—as it should please the Lord, "forever," even through the entire gospel dispensation.

PROMISE OF THE SPIRIT

That Peter understood this promise to cover the Lord's working to the end of time, is set forth in these words: "Repent, and be baptized every one of you in the name of Jesus Christ for the remission of sins, and ye shall receive the gift of the Holy Ghost. For the promise is unto you, and to your children, and to all that are afar off, even as many as the Lord our God shall call." Acts 2:38, 39. Then as long as the Lord calls people to His service, [16] so long is the promise of the Holy Spirit extended to them.

Paul, in writing to the Corinthians, says, "The manifestation of the Spirit is given to every man to profit withal." 1 Corinthians 12:7. The manifestation of the Spirit must refer to its manner of working. The Spirit may and does come to the sinner in his sins, as a *reprover*; but after he yields to the Lord, and it leads the mind to the blessed assurance of God's promises, it is an *approver*. Ephesians 1:13. Then it is that "the Spirit also helpeth our infirmities." Romans 8:26.

Men, in their fallen state, are infirm, "being alienated from the life of God through the ignorance that is in them, because of the blindness of their heart." Ephesians 4:18. "Alienated and enemies in your mind by wicked works." Colossians 1:21. There "are given unto us exceeding great and precious promises; that by these ye might be partakers of the divine nature." 2 Peter 1:4. After yielding to God and becoming partakers of the divine nature, we are recognized as "the sons of God," being "led by the Spirit of God." Romans 8:14. That Spirit dwelling in us quickens (gives life—even the life of God—to) our mortal bodies. Romans 8:11. It then "beareth witness with our spirit, that we are the children of God," and seals us as His. Romans 8:16; 2 Corinthians 1:22. Then the righteousness of the law is fulfilled in us, "who walk not after the flesh, but after the Spirit." Romans 8:4. [17]

THE TEMPLE OF THE SPIRIT

The church of Christ on earth is really a place prepared for the indwelling of the Spirit. The apostle says, "Know ye not that ye are the temple of God, and that the Spirit of God dwelleth in you?" 1 Corinthians 3:16. To the individual members of the church He says, "What? know ye not that your body is the temple of the Holy Ghost which is in you, which ye have of God, and ye are not your own?" 1 Corinthians 6:19. Again, "Ye are the temple of the living God; as God hath said, I will dwell in them, and walk in them." 2 Corinthians 6:16. And once more, "In whom all the building fitly framed together groweth unto an holy temple in the Lord;

in whom ye also are builded together for an habitation of God through the Spirit." Ephesians 2:21, 22. Standing thus, we are "strengthened with might by His Spirit in the inner man." Ephesians 3:16. "Strengthened with all might, according to His glorious power, unto all patience and long-suffering with joyfulness." Colossians 1:11. Thus we may labor, "striving according to His working, which worketh in me mightily." Colossians 1:29.

Manifestation of the Spirit

In Paul's first epistle to the Corinthians he thus speaks of the work of the Spirit, saying: "The manifestation of the Spirit is given to every man to profit withal. For to one is given by the Spirit the word of wisdom; to another the word of knowledge by the same Spirit; to another faith by the same Spirit; [18] to another the gifts of healing by the same Spirit; to another the working of miracles; to another prophecy; to another discerning of spirits; to another divers kinds of tongues; to another the interpretation of tongues; but all these worketh that one and the selfsame Spirit, dividing to every man severally as He will." 1 Corinthians 12:7-11. Those manifestations are all by *one* and the selfsame Spirit. How unlike the communications of Spiritualism, which are from a variety of spirits, many of them being lying spirits!

Paul proceeds in his discourse by comparing the church with the human body, representing the gifts of the Spirit as members of the body, the eyes, ears, hands, etc., saying: "Now hath God set the members every one of them in the body, as it hath pleased Him... And God hath set some in the church, first apostles, secondarily prophets, thirdly teachers, after that miracles, then gifts of healings, helps, governments, diversities of tongues. Are all apostles? are all prophets? are all teachers? are all workers of miracles? have all the gifts of healing? do all speak with tongues? do all interpret? But covet earnestly the best gifts: and yet show I unto you a more excellent way." 1 Corinthians 12:18-31. We here read of the Lord's setting these gifts "in the church;" do we read elsewhere of His setting them out of the church?

Charity, or Love

The more excellent way is not to have a church without the gifts of the Spirit; it is a more excellent [19] way than simply to *"covet"* gifts. That "more excellent way" is fully set forth in 1Corinthians, chapter 13, in the apostle's discourse on charity-fervent love to God, and to our fellow men. Instead of simply coveting some particular gift for ourselves, it is better to seek entire consecration to the Lord—to have His love in our hearts—to "follow after charity, and desire spiritual gifts, but rather that ye may prophesy." 1 Corinthians 14:1. However, this discourse on charity does not dispense with the gifts of the Spirit. We read: "Charity never faileth: but whether there be prophecies, they shall fail; whether there be tongues, they shall cease; whether there be knowledge, it shall vanish away. For we know in part, and we prophesy in part. But when that which is *perfect* is come, then that which is in part shall be done away." 1 Corinthians 13:8-10. By this it is understood that the gift of prophecy may be manifest, as it may please the Lord, until the perfect state shall come. In that state, when the Lord is seen face to face, prophecy will no more be needed. "Now we see through a glass, darkly; but then face to face; now I know in part; but then shall I know even as also I am known." 1 Corinthians 13:12.

Prophecy in the Early Church

On looking through the Acts of the Apostles the fact is apparent that the Lord had many sons and daughters who were favored with divine revelations. In chapter 11 is mentioned the case of Agabus, who [20] predicted the great dearth that was to come on the land of Judea, which prediction moved the Lord's people to provide relief for the poor saints in Judea. Verses 27-30. The exact fulfilment of this prophecy established the faith of the believers in Agabus as a true prophet among them, so that when at Caesarea, nineteen years after, he told them what would be done to Paul at Jerusalem, there seemed to be no question as to the certainty of the fulfilment of his prediction, for they at once besought Paul not to go to Jerusalem. Acts 21:10-12. In the church at Antioch, four prophets are mentioned; namely, Barnabas, Simeon (Niger), Lucius, and Manaen. Acts

13:1. It seems also that Philip, the evangelist, who resided at Caesarea, "had four daughters, virgins," that were prophets. Acts 21:8, 9.

Paul, when writing his epistle to the Ephesians, spoke of the gifts of the Spirit on this wise: "Wherefore He saith, When He ascended up on high, He led captivity captive ["a multitude of captives," margin], and gave gifts unto men... And He gave some, apostles; and some, prophets; and some, evangelists; and some, pastors and teachers; for the perfecting of the saints, for the work of the ministry, for the edifying of the body of Christ; till we all come in ["into," margin] the unity of the faith, and of the knowledge of the Son of God, unto a perfect man, unto the measure of the stature of the fullness of Christ: that we [21] henceforth be no more children, tossed to and fro, and carried about with every wind of doctrine, by the sleight of men, and cunning craftiness, whereby they lie in wait to deceive; but speaking the truth in love, may grow up into Him in all things, which is the Head, even Christ: from whom the whole body fitly joined together and compacted by that which every joint supplieth, according to the effectual working in the measure of every part, maketh increase of the body unto the edifying of itself in love." Chapter 4:8-16.

The Lord gave these gifts for the accomplishment of a certain purpose in His church (perfecting saints and edifying the church), and there still exists a need for such work to be done; who will say that the Lord will not even now, as formerly, manifest those gifts for the same purpose, until probation shall end? It is further seen from the writings of the apostle that he recognizes these gifts as members of the body of Christ; and as such, who has a right to mutilate that body, and say that this or that gift is not now necessary?

THE APOSTASY

We find in the Scriptures that the manifestation of the gift of prophecy is closely allied with obedience to the law of God. When the people faithfully followed the Lord, He favored them with instruction through His prophets. As they fell into sin and departed from His law, they had no vision from God, as already shown. So it is emphatically true, [22] as expressed by Solomon, "Where there is no vision, the people perish: but he that keepeth the law, happy is he." Proverbs 29:18. They are happy, for as they obey the Lord's law, He is pleased to favor them with instruction through His prophets.

Paul said to the elders of the Ephesus church: "For I know this, that after my departing shall grievous wolves enter in among you, not sparing the flock. Also of your own selves shall men arise, speaking perverse things, to draw away disciples after them." Acts 20:29, 30. Also to the church in Thessalonica he said that there should "come a falling away," and "that man of sin be revealed." And of him the apostle said that he should sit "in the temple of God, showing himself that he is God." 2 Thessalonians 2:3, 4.

It is a fact that while the early church maintained their purity, the Lord manifested among them the gifts of His Spirit; but as the apostasy developed, their condition became more and more like that of ancient Israel, of whom He said: "Your iniquities have separated between you and your God, and your sins have hid His face from you, that He will not hear." Isaiah 59:2.

Neander, in his "Church History," thus speaks of the Montanists of the second century: "The Montanists looked upon it expressly as something characteristic of this last epoch of the development of the kingdom of God that, according to the prophecies of Joel then in course of fulfilment, the gifts of the Spirit should indifferently be shed abroad over all classes of Christians of both sexes." "It appears also to have been the doctrine of the Montanists that the season of the last and richest outpouring of the Holy Spirit would form the last age of the church, and precede the second coming of Christ, and be the fulfilment of the prophecy of Joel."—*Rose's Neander, pages 330, 332.*

John Wesley, in speaking of the Montanists, says: "By reflecting on an odd book which I had read in this journey ('The General Delusion of Christians with Regard to Prophecy') I was fully convinced of what I had long suspected: (1) that the Montanists, in the second and third centuries, were real, Scriptural Christians; and (2) that the grand reason why the miraculous gifts were so soon withdrawn, was not only that faith and holiness were well-nigh lost, but that dry, formal, orthodox men began even then to ridicule whatever gifts they had not themselves, and to decry them all, as either madness or imposture."—*Wesley's Journal, volume 3, page 496.*

To the question, "If you allow miracles before the empire became Christian, why not afterward, too?" Mr. Wesley answers, "Because after the empire became Christian, a general corruption both of faith and morals infected the Christian church, which, by that revolution, as St. Jerome says, 'lost as much of her virtue as it had gained of wealth and power.'"—*Wesley's Works, page 706.* [24]

THE REFRESHING

In Acts 3:19-21 is brought to view a time of *refreshing* spoken of in close connection with Christ's second coming. This undoubtedly refers to the same time as that mentioned by the apostle James, when he says: "Be patient therefore, brethren, unto the coming of the Lord. Behold, the husbandman waiteth for the precious fruit of the earth, and hath long patience for it, until he receive the early and latter rain. Be ye also patient; stablish your hearts: for the coming of the Lord draweth nigh." James 5:7, 8.

The early and latter rain is also mentioned by the prophet Joel in connection with his description of the last days. The coming of the "former rain moderately" is called, in the margin of the text, "a teacher of righteousness, according to righteousness." Joel 2:23. The outpouring of the Spirit of God on the day of Pentecost—the coming of the Comforter as a teacher—was comparable to the "former rain," which caused the newly sown seed of the husbandman to take root and grow. So in the ripening of the harvest of the earth, just before the end, the Husbandman—our heavenly Father (John 15:1)—is waiting for the "latter rain," the "refreshing," to aid in ripening off the harvest of the earth. The Lord has said by His prophet, "Ask ye of the Lord rain in the time of the latter rain; so the Lord shall make bright clouds, and give them showers of rain, to every [25] one grass in the field." Zechariah 10:1. And thus will be fulfilled His promise: "Then shall we know, if we follow on to know the Lord: His going forth is prepared as the morning; and He shall come unto us as the rain, as the latter and former rain unto the earth." Hosea 6:3.

Perilous Times

The time immediately preceding the second coming of Christ is presented as perilous, as a time of the working of Satan in mighty power, and also a time in which the Lord's people will be in a special sense "kept by the power of God through faith unto salvation ready to be revealed in the *last time*." 1 Peter 1:5. Why should it be a thing improbable for the Lord to pour out in a special manner His Spirit to instruct, strengthen, and keep His people from the wiles of Satan in that trying time?

In writing to Timothy, Paul says, "This know also, that in the last days perilous times shall come." He then enumerates eighteen sins to be found among a people having the "form of godliness, but denying the *power* thereof." Of these he says: "Now as Jannes and Jambres withstood Moses, so do these also resist the truth... Their folly shall be manifest unto all men, as theirs also was." 2 Timothy 3:1-9. Jannes and Jambres were chief magicians of Pharaoh, who sought to resist the work of the Lord through Moses by counterfeit miracles. The Lord, by the hand of His servant [26] Moses, wrought in a manner that the magicians could not counterfeit. Exodus 7:11; 8:18, 19. It is seen, then, that as the end is nearing, and Satan works in power, the Lord gives showers of blessings to His people, thus defeating the purpose of Satan. So they are kept by the *power* of God, and the folly of counterfeit workers made manifest.

Final Deliverance

In many scriptures the Lord compares the deliverance of His people from Egypt, with the final deliverance of His saints. As a sample see Ezekiel 20:35-37. One feature that was connected with the deliverance of Israel, is mentioned by the prophet Hosea when he says, "By a prophet the Lord brought Israel out of Egypt, and by a prophet was he preserved." Hosea 12:13. So if there is a similarity in the last deliverance to that from Egypt, we may look for the gift of prophecy to be connected with the preparation for the deliverance.

LAW AND PROPHET'S MESSAGE

In the following words of Isaiah is shown to the prophet what is to be expected in the last days: "Now go, write it before them in a table, and note it in a book, that it may be for the time to come forever and ever ["the latter day," margin, Heb.]: that this is a rebellious people, lying children, children that will not hear the law of the Lord: which say to the seers, See not; and to the prophets, Prophesy not unto us right things, speak unto us smooth things, prophesy deceits: get you out of the [27] way, turn aside out of the path, cause the Holy One of Israel to cease from before us." Isaiah 30:8-11. By reference to 1 Samuel 9:9, we learn that a *seer* and a prophet mean one and the same, for there we read that "he that is now called a prophet was beforetime called a seer"—one who had visions from God and prophesied. The force, then, of the above scripture is that the gift of prophecy will be connected with the proclamation of God's law in the last days. This the masses will reject, because they do not like reproof, preferring a smooth path.

SPIRIT OF PROPHECY

In the New Testament, where Paul is speaking of the people waiting for Christ's second coming, he says: "I thank my God always on your behalf, for the grace of God which is given you by Jesus Christ; that in everything ye are enriched by Him, in all utterance, and in all knowledge; even as the testimony of Christ was confirmed in you: so that ye come behind in no gift; waiting for the coming of our Lord Jesus Christ: who shall also confirm you unto the end, that ye may be blameless in the day of our Lord Jesus Christ." 1 Corinthians 1:4-8. Thus all the gifts are to be manifest among that people who stand at last prepared to meet Christ in peace at His coming.

From this it also appears that one gift is singled out, the confirmation of which prepares the way for *all* the gifts to be developed in the church. That one gift he calls *the testimony of Jesus*. To ascertain [28] the meaning of this scripture, we will compare it with others. In Revelation, chapter 12, after the persecution of the Dark Ages, we find the apostle speaking thus of the last of the church in her probationary state: "And the dragon was wroth with the woman, and went to make war with the *remnant* of her seed, which keep the commandments of God, and have the testimony of Jesus Christ." Verse 17. The *remnant* of the church is the last of the church in its probation here. This is seen in Joel's prophecy of the Lord's people just before the great and terrible day of the Lord. In the preparation for that day He says salvation shall be "in the *remnant* whom the Lord shall call." Joel 2:32. This remnant will have war made on them for keeping all of God's commandments, and for having manifested among them the *testimony* of Jesus.

By looking in Revelation, chapter 19, we get a Scripture definition of the "testimony of Jesus." This is John's account, given while in vision on the isle of Patmos. He mistook the beautiful angel that was before him, for an object for him to worship, and said: "I fell at his feet to worship him. And he said unto me, See thou do it not: I am thy fellow servant, and of thy brethren that have the testimony of Jesus: worship God: for the testimony of Jesus is the spirit of prophecy." Verse 10. We now have an inspired definition that the testimony of Jesus is the *spirit of prophecy*.

When we have the right definition of a word or [29] phrase,, it is proper to substitute the definition in the sentence. Substituting thus in 1 Corinthians 1:6, 7, the text would read, "The spirit of prophecy was confirmed in you: so that ye come behind in no gift; waiting for the coming of our Lord Jesus Christ." And in Revelation 12:17 it would read that the dragon went to make war with the remnant who "keep the commandments of God, and have the spirit of prophecy." We see, then, that the remnant church, the members of which will be keeping all of God's commandments, are to have the gift of prophecy among them, and that that gift is to lead out in preparing the way so that all the gifts will at last be manifested among the people who are waiting for Christ's coming. Thus, as the Lord's people return to obedience, to the keeping of all His commandments, the gift of prophecy is restored to His people.

Prophesyings

In the first epistle of Paul to the Thessalonians, chapter 4, he speaks of Christ's second coming, the resurrection of the righteous, and the change of the living saints. In the fifth chapter he shows that that day will come upon the masses as a thief in the night. He says, however, "But ye, brethren, are not in darkness, that that day should overtake you as a thief." 1 Thessalonians 5:4. That people who will be found watching for Christ's coming, whom He calls "children of light," He exhorts as follows: "Rejoice evermore. Pray without ceasing. [30]

In everything give thanks: for this is the will of God in Christ Jesus concerning you. Quench not the Spirit. Despise not *prophesyings*. Prove all things; hold fast that which is good." 1 Thessalonians 5:16-21.

What is more consistent than to expect the Lord to teach directly His people who are to pass through the perils of the last days and be prepared to meet the Saviour in peace at His coming? It is that point of time to which the patriarchs, and the true prophets of all past time, have looked with intense interest, when the conflict of ages, the controversy between sin and righteousness, is to close, and the age for which all other ages were made is to be brought in. It can not be that God, who is abundant in mercy, will refrain from specially instructing His people. Thanks be to God, He has not left this as a matter of supposition; for He will guide His people by the spirit of prophecy, as the Scriptures clearly teach.

Proving the Gift

There is no surer way to prove a prophetic gift than by comparing it with the description of such gifts as were manifested in Scripture times, and testing it by the rules therein given. There are seven complete rules given in the Scriptures by which we may know a genuine gift of prophecy. These are noted in the second part of this book.

The gifts, and especially the gift of prophecy, have a part to act in bringing the church into "unity" and harmony. "God is not the author [31] of confusion, but of peace." In fact, the gathering of a people from the confused elements of earth, and the various nations of the world, to move forward as one, is one of the best evidences of a genuine work of the Lord.

The true gift of prophecy will not give any revelation to take the place of the Scriptures. While it may shed light on the Scriptures, leading the people into the "unity of the faith," its great work will be that of counsel, and instructions how to live, act, and move in these last days of peril.

Conclusion

The question may arise, What need have we of the gift of prophecy? We have the Old Testament, the words of Christ and His apostles, and the Revelation. Did not Christ forbid more prophesying when He said, "If any man shall add unto these things, God shall add unto him the plagues that are written in this book" (Revelation 22:18)? We reply, Should the Lord bestow the gift of prophecy upon a person for the instruction and guidance of His people, it would not be an addition to the book of Revelation.

After the Lord had spoken from Sinai, and given the law to His people, with statutes and judgments, they might have said, We have the Lord's word now, and do not need prophets. The Lord knew best; and as we have seen, He multiplied visions and similitudes by His prophets for the instruction of that people. This did not add to nor take from [32] that already given them; but it did show them where they were led astray by circumstances peculiar to their time. These revelations shed also a clearer luster on the truths they had already received, and made bright the light relating to the promised Messiah and His glory.

With the subject of the gifts opened before us in the Scriptures, with the fact so plainly manifest that the gift of prophecy is to be connected with the last work of God's people in probationary time, and with rules placed in our hands by which to test such gifts, is it not important that the mind be divested of prejudice, not "despising" such a gift, but, on the contrary, looking for a work of this character that is to be developed in these last days? [33]

Part 2

"FOR yourselves know perfectly that the day of the Lord so cometh as a thief in the night... But ye, brethren, are not in darkness, that that day should overtake you as a thief. Ye are all the children of light, and the children of the day: we are not of the night, nor of darkness." 11 Thessalonians 5:2-5.

To the people who are not in the dark concerning the coming of the Lord the apostle gives the following weighty exhortations: "Quench not the Spirit. Despise not prophesyings. Prove all things; hold fast that which is good." Verses 19-21.

It is evident from this language that if the Spirit of the Lord is allowed to work as God designs, there will be among the believers in the second advent, *good* and *true* manifestations of the prophetic gift. Murdock's Syriac translation of this text reads, "Despise not prophesying." Greenfield, in his Greek lexicon, gives as the meaning of the word here rendered "prophesyings," "the exercise of the gift of prophecy in this sense. 1 Thessalonians 5:21." With this, also, agree the lexicons of Parkhurst, Robinson, and Liddell and Scott.

When writing to the Corinthians the apostle speaks of those who will be waiting for Christ's second coming, and says, "Ye come behind in no gift; waiting for the coming of our Lord Jesus Christ: who shall also confirm you unto the end, [34] that ye may be blameless in the day of our Lord Jesus Christ." 1 Corinthians 1:7, 8.

Of the church waiting for Christ's second coming we read in Revelation: "And the dragon [the devil] was wroth with the woman [the church], and went to make war with the remnant of her seed, which keep the commandments of God, and have the testimony of Jesus Christ." Revelation 12:17. This phrase, "testimony of Jesus," is clearly defined in Revelation 19:10, *"The testimony of Jesus is the spirit of prophecy."* Here, then, is the last of the church in her probationary state, two features being prominent in her work,—the keeping of all the commandments of God, and having the spirit of prophecy.

In Part One was presented quite fully the Scriptural evidence for spiritual gifts in the gospel church, as well as the proofs that the gifts will be found with the *last* phase of the church in her probationary state. It was not the Lord that put the *gifts* out of the church, but the apostasy of the church—separating from God—which limited these manifestations. All the way along the Lord has been ready to show forth His power and His gifts with those who have fully sought Him.

That it was the Lord's pleasure to manifest His power is shown in the great gospel commission, where the Saviour said, "And, lo, I am with you alway, even unto the end of the world." Matthew 28:20. In Mark's record of the same commission a [35] statement is given of some of the ways the Lord's presence among His servants would be known: "These signs shall follow them that believe; In My name shall they cast out devils; they shall speak with new tongues; they shall take up serpents; and if they drink any deadly thing, it shall not hurt them; they shall lay hands on the sick, and they shall recover." Mark 16:17, 18.

There were some wonderful displays of the Lord's power and manifestations of the gift of prophecy during the Reformation of the sixteenth century, and in the times following. D'Aubigne speaks of the prophecies of John Huss. Charles Buck, in his religious anecdotes, tells of the prophesying of George Wishart, in 1546. John Wesley, in his works, tells of the prophecies of Jonathan Pyrah, and their fulfilment. Elder J. B. Finley, in his autobiography, tells of a remarkable vision and healing in his own person, in the summer of 1842. The *Christian Advocate* (Methodist) published an interesting account of a remarkable vision and its results, as given to Doctor Bond, of that church, during his ministry. These were tokens, to those humbly seeking the Lord, that He had not changed, and that He still would speak to His people through the prophetic gift.

About 1833, but more especially since 1840, a message has been sounding through the earth proclaiming the coming of Christ near at hand, "even at the doors." In connection with this proclamation [36] the Lord has been pleased to manifest the power of His Spirit in various ways, and in a marked manner. In many instances, not only in America, but in other countries, the Lord has been gracious to His people who have been engaged in heralding the glad tidings of our returning Lord, by speaking to them through the gift of prophecy. Attention is here called to some instances of this character in America.

The first to be noticed is that of a godly man,—a well-educated and talented minister by the name of William Foye, who resided in Boston, Massachusetts. At two different times during the year 1842, the Lord came so near to him that he was wrapped in holy vision. One of these occasions was on January 18, and the other was on February 4. By invitation he went from city to city to tell of the wonderful things he had seen; and in order to accommodate the vast crowds that assembled to hear him, large halls were secured, where he related to thousands what had been shown him of the heavenly world, the loveliness of the New Jerusalem and the angelic hosts. When dwelling upon the tender, compassionate love of Jesus for poor sinners, he exhorted the unconverted to seek God, and scores responded to his tender entreaties.

Mr. Foye's work continued until the year 1844, near the close of the twenty-three hundred days of Daniel 8:14. Then he was favored with another manifestation of the Holy Spirit,—a third vision was [37] given,—one which he did not understand. In this was shown him a pathway of the people of God through to the heavenly city. He saw a great platform, on which multitudes of people gathered. Occasionally one would drop through this platform out of sight, and of such a one it was said to him, "Apostatized." Then he saw the people rise to a second platform, and some of these also dropped through the platform out of sight; and finally a third platform appeared, which extended to the gates of the holy city. A great company gathered with those who had advanced to this platform. As he expected the Lord Jesus to come in a very short time, he failed to recognize the fact that a third message was to follow the first and second messages of Revelation 14. Consequently the vision, to him, was inexplicable, and he ceased public speaking. After the close of the prophetic period, in the year 1845, he heard Miss E. G. Harmon relate the same vision, with the explanation that "the first and second messages had been given, and that a third was to follow." Soon after this, however, Mr. Foye sickened and died.

Another instance of the manifestation of the gift of prophecy is found in the case of a young man that resided in Poland, Maine, by the name of Hazen Foss. He was a man of fine appearance, pleasing address, with a good academic education. In the month of September, 1844, about six weeks before the close of the twenty-three hundred days, [38] the Lord gave him a vision, in which he, like Mr. Foye, saw the "three platforms" in the heavenly pathway. Some messages of warning to individuals were also given him, which he was instructed to deliver. In connection with this he saw the trials and persecutions that would follow if he was faithful in relating what had been shown to him. As he was also expecting the Lord to come "in a few more days" (as they then sang), he did not understand the *third step* ("platform") in the journey; and, shrinking from the cross, he refused to relate the vision. The view was repeated to him; and in addition, warning was given that if he still refused to tell what had been shown him, the burden would be taken from him, and given to one of the *weakest* of the Lord's children, one who would faithfully narrate what God would reveal. Again he refused. A third vision was given him, a very short one, in which he was told that he was released, and saw the person upon whom the Lord had laid the burden, "one of the *weakest* of the weak, who would do the Lord's bidding."

This startled the young man, who at once appointed a meeting on McGuire Hill, Poland, Maine, for the purpose of relating what had been revealed to him. The people crowded together to see and hear him. He carefully related his experience,—how he had refused to relate what the Lord had shown him, and what would result from the refusal. "Now," said he, "I will tell you the vision." But, [39] alas!! it was too late! It had gone from him. Not a word could he recall. He wrung his hands in anguish, saying: "God has fulfilled His word. He has taken the vision from me. I am a lost man." From that time the man lived without hope. He died in 1896.

About two months after the close of the twenty-three hundred days (about January 1, 1845), Miss Ellen G. Harmon, of Portland, Maine, then a little past seventeen years of age, began to receive revelations from the Lord. She was at that time in a very critical condition of health, being, indeed, as had been told to Foss regarding the instrument God would choose, "THE WEAKEST OF THE WEAK." From a wound received when about nine years of age, she nearly bled to death, and ever afterward was unable to attend school. For several weeks before her first revelation she had scarcely been able to speak above a whisper. One physician diagnosed her case as dropsical consumption, with the right lung decayed, and the left one considerably diseased; and to aggravate her condition, her heart also was affected. All this made her recovery doubtful; in fact, he thought she could live but a very short time at most, and was liable to drop away at any moment. It was with great difficulty that she could breathe when lying down, and at night she could obtain rest only by being bolstered up in bed in an almost sitting posture. Frequent spells of coughing and hemorrhages from the lungs had [40] greatly reduced her physical strength. Her weight at that time was only seventy pounds.

In this weakened condition, she was instructed, in vision, to go and relate to others what the Lord had made known to her. She was directed to go to Poland, Maine,—the place where Foss had failed when trying to relate the vision given to him. Here she related what the Lord had shown her. In an adjoining room, Foss heard the narration; and after meeting he remarked to others, "The vision Ellen related is as near like what was shown to me as two persons could tell the same thing." The next morning, on seeing Miss Harmon, he said, "That is the instrument on whom the Lord has laid the burden." To Miss Harmon he said, "Be faithful in bearing the burden laid upon you, and in relating the testimonies the Lord shall give you, and you will get through to the kingdom;" and then, in anguish, he said, "O, I am a lost man!"

The gift of prophecy, as manifested through Miss Harmon (now Mrs. E. G. White, she having been married to Elder James White in August, 1846), has been connected with the third angel's message for about sixty-five years.

The students of Scripture prophecies have ever claimed that "when the time comes for the fulfilment of a prophecy, the genuine fulfilment is there, and not a counterfeit." The Lord's time came for the third angel's message,— for a people to arise teaching the observance of all the commandments [41] of God,—a message with which should be connected the spirit of prophecy. There is just such a message now being given to the world, and the gift of prophecy is connected with it; not to give a new revelation to take the place of the Scriptures, but simplifying and making clear the truths taught therein, and urging the importance of more earnest study of the sacred Word.

"The spirits of the prophets are subject to the prophets." 1 Corinthians 14:32. The same Spirit that actuates one true prophet of God controls and actuates another. So in the true manifestation of the Holy Spirit there must be a similarity in the visions now given, to those described in the Bible. It may be well, however, briefly to notice some Scriptural accounts of true visions from God, comparing them with the *"open visions"*—visions given before the people—of Mrs. E. G. White.

It has been the privilege of the writer to witness this manifestation through Mrs. White nearly fifty times during the last fifty-eight years, and to learn, in the year 1858, from the lips of those conversant, with the beginning of this manifestation through her, the history of the same.

It may be well, however, before making the comparisons, to describe the manifestation itself as seen in Mrs. White. In the particulars which I now endeavor to give, there was never a variation in all the numerous visions that the writer has witnessed. As the blessing of the Lord's Spirit would fall upon [42] her in power, she would give three shouts, speaking the word "Glory!" The first shout, as nearly as can be described, sounded as if coming from the upper part of the room, and was accompanied by thrills of the power of the Lord, affecting all present whose hearts were susceptible to the Spirit of God. The second shout sounded still farther off, and the impress of the Spirit on those present was deeper. The third shout resembled that of a voice in the distance, like one just going out of hearing. With this the presence of the Spirit would be felt in a still greater degree, reminding one of the day of Pentecost, when the Spirit "filled all the house where they were sitting." Acts 2:2.

After the third shout, for half a minute or more, there was a complete loss of strength. If the power of the Spirit came upon her when standing, she appeared gradually to settle down to the floor, as if being gently let down by unseen hands. When fairly in vision, the action of the heart and pulse was natural, but the closest tests of medical men failed to discover a particle of breath in her body. The color of the countenance was natural, the eyes were open, always looking upward, not with a vacant stare, neither in a stationary position, but turning from side to side in different directions, the only difference from the natural look being like that of one looking intently at some object in the distance. After a moment of weakness, a *superhuman* power came upon her. While she would sometimes rise to [43] her feet, and walk about the room, gracefully moving her arms to the right or left, yet in whatever position the arm might be placed, it was impossible for strong men to move it an inch.

When we look at the Scripture record of visions given to God's servants, we find many particulars relative to the physical condition of the entranced person. In the case of Paul, as recorded in his letter to the Corinthians, he says, "I will come to visions and revelations of the Lord." 2 Corinthians 12:1. That he speaks of himself and his own visions is evident from the seventh verse, where he says, "And lest I should be exalted above measure through the abundance of the revelations, there was given to me a thorn in the flesh, the messenger of Satan to buffet me, lest I should be exalted above measure."

Paul says of his visions: "I knew a man in Christ above fourteen years ago, (whether in the body, I can not tell; or whether out of the body, I can not tell: God knoweth;) such an one caught up to the third heaven. And I knew such a man, (whether in the body, or out of the body, I can not tell: God knoweth;) how that he was caught up into Paradise, and heard unspeakable words, which it is not lawful ["not possible," margin] for a man to utter." Verses 2-4.

When the veil was drawn back, and Paul was permitted to look upon heavenly scenes, it appeared to him as if he went up to heaven. The same was true in John's case. Revelation 4:1. Paul was lost to [44] everything around him. While the vision continued, he knew nothing of his surroundings, and so he could only testify of what he saw while in vision.

The closest tests applied to Mrs. White while in vision have led the most skeptical to decide that she was oblivious to all her surroundings. Pricking the hands with needles would not occasion the slightest resistance. A lighted candle brought suddenly so near her eyes as to singe her eyebrows, or even the tip end of the finger touched to the pupil of the eye, failed to produce the least resistance, or to cause her to flinch. Those thus experimenting have exclaimed, "She does not know anything of what is taking place around her."

The next comparison will be in the case of Daniel's vision as recorded in chapter 10. He said to the angel: "For how can the servant of this my lord talk with this my lord? for as for me, straightway there remained no strength in me, neither is there breath left in me. Then there came again and touched me one like the appearance of a man [by reference to Daniel 9:21 we learn that the one who appeared to him before was the *man* Gabriel], and he strengthened me, and said, O man greatly beloved, fear not: peace be unto thee, be strong, yea, be strong. And when he had spoken unto me, I was strengthened, and said, Let my lord speak; for thou hast strengthened me." Verses 17-19.

Here are *five* points in the description of his vision: loss of strength; sees an angel; the angel [45] puts his hand upon him; he is supernaturally strengthened; and no breath in his body, though he is talking to the angel at the same time.

As before stated, the first thing, as Mrs. White goes into vision, is loss of consciousness of earthly things, and loss of strength. The first thing she sees is a bright, glorious angel, who lays his hand upon her. She is then clothed with strength, sometimes rising to her feet, walking about the room with a great Bible open on her left arm; and while her eyes are turned upward, and away from the book, with her right hand the leaves of the book are turned from page to page, the fingers pointing to texts, which she repeats verbatim, though her eyes are never once turned toward them. While thus talking and quoting Scripture, the closest test of skilful physicians has failed to detect breath in her body. Thus in these five particulars, her visions are precisely like the visions of Daniel.

While she is in vision, physicians have held a lighted candle as close to her lips as possible without burning her; and notwithstanding she was speaking with much force in the voice, not a single flicker was made in the blaze of the candle. Such a test was made by two physicians in Rochester, New York, June 24, 1854. After the experiment, they said: "That settles it! There is not a particle of breath in that woman's body!" On another occasion, in 1853, a physician seeing her recover her breath on coming out of vision, said, "The action is precisely [46] like that of the new-born infant drawing its first breath, and is POSITIVE *proof* that while in the vision she has not been breathing."

Another feature in connection with visions recorded in the Bible is found in the case of Balaam. We read: "Balaam the son of Beor hath said, and the man whose eyes are open ["who had his eyes shut, but now opened," margin, Hebrew] hath said: he hath said, which heard the words of God, which saw the vision of the Almighty, falling into a trance, but having his eyes open." Numbers 24:3, 4, 16. Boothroyd translates it, in verses 4, 16, "entranced, but with open eyes." Spurrell's translation, margin, "entranced with eyes rolled upward." As previously said, Mrs. White's eyes are always open during the entire vision. We have now presented seven points in which this manifestation through Mrs. White is in accord with Bible visions.

The question will now naturally arise, How can a person talk without breath? Such a phenomenon is a miracle of God's power. Indeed, it is thrilling to listen to the voice of an angel speaking through the vocal organs of a human being. How did the ancient prophets speak without breath? In Peter's second epistle we read, "For the prophecy came not in old time by the will of man: but holy men of God spake as they were moved by the Holy Ghost." 2 Peter 1:21. "Men had utterance from God, being moved by the Holy Spirit." Dean Alford's New Testament. The Spirit of God did the talking through the prophet. [47]

We will look at another testimony, one in regard to David's prophecies: "The Spirit of the Lord *spake* by me, and His word was *in my tongue*." 2 Samuel 23:2. The Spirit of God did the speaking, using the tongue of David. Another testimony concerning David's prophesying is found in Peter's testimony: "Men and brethren, this scripture must needs have been fulfilled, which *the Holy Ghost* by the mouth of David *spake* before concerning Judas, which was guide to them that took Jesus." Acts 1:16. The Holy Spirit spoke, using David's mouth. So, in the case of Mrs. White, when in holy vision, although there is no breath, the Holy Spirit speaks in an audible voice, using her organs of speech.

A ninth point of comparison is in relation to the writing of what has been previously shown in vision. In the first book of Chronicles we have an account of David preparing for his son Solomon to build the temple at Jerusalem. He speaks of many particulars concerning the building,—its chambers, treasuries, parlors, furniture, and service. Of this he says it was "the pattern of all that he had by the Spirit." 1 Chronicles 28:12. The Lord had shown him, by the Spirit, as He showed to Moses, a *pattern* of this building that was *"a shadow* of heavenly things." And everything must be made as exact as the pattern. This must all be written out for Solomon's instruction. David tells us *how* this was done. "All this, said David, the Lord made me understand in writing by His hand upon me, even all the works [48] of this pattern." 1 Chronicles 28:19. The Lord had shown him these things in vision. As he set himself to write them, the Spirit of God brought them clearly before his mind, and thus he wrote them out.

It is in this manner that Mrs. White is enabled to commit to writing the many things previously shown her in vision. She says, "I have been aroused from my sleep with a vivid sense of subjects previously presented to my mind, and have written, at midnight, letters that have gone across the continent [of America], and arriving at a crisis, have saved great disaster to the cause of God."

Again, she says: "Sometimes, when special dangers threaten the cause of God or particular individuals, a communication comes to me from the Lord, either in a dream or a vision of the night, and these cases are brought vividly to my mind. I hear a voice saying to me, 'Arise and *write*; these souls are in peril.' I obey the movings of the Spirit of God, and my pen traces their true condition."—Testimonies for the Church 5:685.

Practical Working of the Gift

We now have *nine* points in which Mrs. White's visions are like those described in the Bible. It may be well to note next the harmony of the practical working of her gift with like work described in the Scriptures.

In considering the manifestation of the gifts of the Spirit, it is well to keep in mind the order of the development of the gifts, as the Lord has marked [49] it out in His Word. Paul refers to this order in his letter to the Corinthians, where he says, "God hath set some in the church, *first* apostles, *secondarily* prophets." 1 Corinthians 12:28.

When comparing these gifts, he says, "Wherefore tongues are for a sign, not to them that believe, but to them that believe not: but prophesying serveth not for them that believe not, but for them which believe." 1 Corinthians 14:22.

From this statement it is evident that the Lord's order is that His special messages to the world shall be brought forth from His word; and accordingly He moves men to search the Scriptures, and to go forth as apostles, burdened with the Lord's messages, proclaiming them from the Bible, which has stood the test of ages. Not all ministers are classed as apostles; but that term seems to be applied to those who lead out in a reform or a new development of gospel truth. As believers are raised up, the gift of prophecy comes in, "secondarily," accomplishing its part "for the perfecting of the saints, for the work of the ministry, for the edifying of the body of Christ." Ephesians 4:12.

The work of Miss E. G. Harmon, under the guidance of the prophetic gift, from January, 1845, to the spring of 1846, almost eighteen months, was with the "believers" in Christ's near coming, with whom she had previously associated. After the close of the twenty-three hundred days (October 22, 1844), until the cause of their disappointment and [50] the nature of the event that then occurred should be understood, there would be danger of the believers' drifting into erroneous views, or giving up entirely their past experience. Her message to such was: "The past movement was of God. Hold fast your faith. The Lord has still a work for His people. Study the Bible. Search the Word, and you will find the light."

While Miss Harmon was busily engaged in one part of New England, Elder Joseph Bates, who was consecrated to God, and was a man of great faith (not acquainted with Miss Harmon), was working in another part, bringing forth from the Scriptures the light of the Sabbath truth and the third angel's message. His work was to raise up believers in these truths. In fact, it was from him that, in 1846, both Miss Harmon and Elder James White received the Sabbath truth. She never had a vision on the Sabbath question until after the Bible evidences for the Sabbath had been given her by Elder Bates.

In the fall of 1846 (after Miss Harmon's marriage to Elder James White), as believers in the third angel's message and the Sabbath were raised up, the Lord's time came for the gift of prophecy to be connected with the third angel's message. Elder Bates became fully convinced that the manifestations of Mrs. White were from heaven. From that time this prophetic gift has acted its part for "believers," "for the work of the ministry," and for the "edifying [building up] of the body [church] [51] of Christ." So we say of the gift of prophecy, as connected with the third angel's message, that it *started right*, and has wrought in a manner in harmony with God's order of placing His gifts in the church.

COMPARISON

In Paul's first letter to the Corinthians he speaks of one coming in where the gift of prophecy is in exercise, "Thus are the secrets of his heart made manifest; and so falling down on his face he will worship God, and report that God is in you of a truth." 1 Corinthians 14:25. Boothroyd's translation reads, "God is among you."

As an illustration of this text, attention is called to a vision given to Mrs. White, and witnessed by the writer. The first Sabbath in October, 1852, in Rochester, New York, she in vision saw a man who, so she told us, was traveling away from home on business. He had much to say about the law of God and the Sabbath, but was at the same time breaking one of the ten commandments. She said he was a person whom she had never met, yet she believed she would see him sometime, as his case had been unfolded to her. One of the Rochester company, whom Mrs. White had never seen, was at that time in Michigan. About six weeks after this vision, he returned to Rochester. As soon as Mrs. White looked upon his countenance, she said to one of the sisters, "That is the man I saw in vision of whom I told you." The vision being related to this man [52] in the presence of his wife and other persons, Mrs. White said to him, as Nathan said to David, "Thou art the man." The brother at once dropped upon his face before his wife, and said, "God is with you of a truth." Then, still upon his knees, he made a full confession of his course while in Michigan, in violating the seventh commandment, as revealed to Mrs. White, who was over five hundred miles away at the time. He frankly told how he had been trapped into sin, and said it was the first transgression of the kind in his life, and should be the last.

Another Comparison

Will be a feature connected with the vision of Daniel, recorded in chapter 10 of his prophecy. We read: "I Daniel alone saw the vision: for the men that were with me saw not the vision; but a great quaking fell upon them, so that they fled to hide themselves." Verse 7. These men in company with Daniel were Chaldeans, and worshipers of idols. When the power of God came upon Daniel, they were as anxious to get away from it as was Adam, after his transgression, to hide from God's presence.

A parallel circumstance occurred in Parkville, Michigan, January 12, 1861. It was the day of the dedication of the Parkville meeting-house, and a large audience had assembled. Elder White and his wife, Elder J. H. Waggoner, and the writer were present. At the close of the service, Mrs. White gave an exhortation, and the blessing of God rested [53] upon her in a remarkable degree. After sitting down, she was taken off in vision, and remained seated. There was present a Doctor Brown, a hale, strong man physically, who was a Spiritualist medium. As was afterward learned, he had said that Mrs. White's visions were the same as spirit mediumship, and that if she had one where he was, he could bring her out of it in one minute. Elder White gave an invitation for all who desired to do so to come forward and by examination satisfy themselves as to her condition while in vision. Some one said, "Doctor, go ahead, and do as you said you would." Elder White then asked: "Is there a doctor in the house? We always like to have physicians examine Mrs. White in vision." The doctor started quite bravely; but before he got half way to Mrs. White, he turned deathly pale and shook like a leaf. He was urged to go on and make the examination. As soon as this was completed, he made his way rapidly to the door, and seized hold of the knob to go out. Those standing by prevented him, saying: "Go back, and do what you said you would do. Bring that woman out of the vision." Elder White, seeing the doctor trying to get out of the door, said, "Will the doctor please report to the audience?" He replied, "Her heart and pulse are regular, but there is not a particle of breath in her body." Then, in great agitation, he again grasped the knob of the door. The people near him said, "Doctor, what is it?" He replied, *"God only* [54] *knows;; let me out of this house."* And out he went. It was evident that the spirit that influenced him as a medium was no more at rest in the presence of the power that controlled Mrs. White in vision than were the demoniacs who inquired of the Saviour, "Art Thou come hither to torment us before the time?" And like the Chaldeans mentioned above, he fled to "hide" himself.

Angelic Influence Illustrated

In the Bible we have numerous accounts of the power and influence of angels. Ferocious animals have been tamed by their presence, as in the case of the hungry lions when Daniel was thrown into their midst. Those lions were calmed by the presence of an angel, and became as peaceable as domestic animals.

By way of comparison, we cite an instance where the influence of the angel who is ever present when Mrs. White is in vision, calmed the temper of an unruly, vicious horse. In the fall of 1846 Elder and Mrs. White wished to go from Topsham to Poland, Maine, a distance of about thirty miles. Elder White obtained the use of a partly-broken colt, and a two-seated market-wagon, which was constructed without a dashboard. There was a step across the front of the wagon, and an iron step from the shafts. It was necessary that extreme care be taken in driving the colt; for if the lines or anything touched his flanks, he would instantly kick furiously; and he had to be held in continually with a "taut rein" [55] to keep him from running. The owner of this colt lived in Poland. As Elder White had been used to managing unbroken colts, he thought he would have no serious trouble with this one. Had he known, however, that during its frantic demonstrations it had previously killed two men, one by crushing him against the rocks by the roadside, he might have been less confident.

On this occasion there were four persons in the wagon,—Elder White and his wife on the front seat, and Elder Bates and a Mr. Israel Damon on the back seat. While Elder White was giving his utmost care to keep the horse under control, Mrs. White was conversing about the truth, when suddenly the power of God came down upon the company, and she was taken off in vision while seated in the wagon. The moment she shouted, "Glory!" as she went into vision, the colt stopped perfectly still, and dropped his head, looking like a sleepy old horse. At the same time, Mrs. White arose, and, with her eyes turned upward, stepped over the front of the wagon, down onto the shafts, with her hand on the colt's haunches. Elder Bates called out to Elder White, "The colt will kick that woman to death." Elder White replied, "The Lord has the colt in charge now; I do not wish to interfere." The colt stood as quietly as an old horse. By the roadside was a bank about six feet high, and beyond, next the fence, was a grassy place. Elder Bates said that the bank was steeper than the roof of a [56] house,, and that they could not ascend it. Mrs. White, with her eyes still upward, not once looking down, went up the bank as readily as if she was going up a flight of stairs. She walked back and forth on the grass-plot for a few minutes, describing the beauties of the new earth. Then, with her eyes in the same posture, she came down the bank, and walking up to the wagon, stepped upon the step of the shafts, again laying her hand on the colt. She then stepped on the shafts, and into the wagon. The moment she sat down upon the seat, she came out of the vision; and that instant the horse, without any indication from the driver, started up, ready to go on his way, but completely tamed.

While Mrs. White was out of the wagon, Elder White thought he would test the horse, and see if he were really tame. At first he just touched him with the whip; at other times the horse would have responded with a kick, but he did not move. Elder White then struck him quite a blow, then harder, and still harder. The colt paid no attention whatever to the blows, but seemed as harmless as the lions whose mouths the angel shut the night Daniel spent in their den. "It was a solemn place," said Elder Bates, "and it was evident that the same power that produced the vision, for the time being subdued the wild nature of the colt." They had no more trouble with the colt in completing the journey. This I have stated as related to me by Elders Bates and White. [57]

Satan's Plans Defeated

In the sixth chapter of the second book of Kings is found a narration of an interesting incident: "The king of Syria warred against Israel, and took counsel with his servants, saying, In such and such a place shall be my camp. And the man of God [Elisha] sent unto the king of Israel, saying, Beware that thou pass not such a place; for thither the Syrians are come down. And the king of Israel sent to the place which the man of God told him and warned him of, and saved himself there, not once nor twice." Verses 8-10. It is evident, from this account, that Satan was working through the Syrians to destroy the Israelites, but the word of the Lord, by the prophet, exposed his satanic work.

The character of the revelations given to Mrs. White has been, from the first, to warn the church of the devices and schemes of Satan, and to point out the way of escape from his wiles and snares. This has been apparent many times in the counsels and warnings sent to those in responsible places in the various institutions. From time to time words of caution have come stating that if certain plans contemplated, or already entered upon, are carried out, it will be disastrous to the cause, and that such and such is a scheme of Satan's suggesting. Then the proper course to pursue has been given, and, when followed, has saved the Lord's servants from defeat, and His cause from disaster. [58]

Dorchester Vision

I call to mind a circumstance connected with Mrs. White's first visit to Massachusetts, in the spring of 1845, as related to me by Bro. Otis Nichols. She first met with the company in Dorchester in the spacious rooms of the home of Mr. Otis Nichols. A company of Adventist believers was in Boston, about seven miles from Dorchester, and a larger company was at Randolph, eight or nine miles in the opposite direction. Mr. Nichols was anxious that Miss Harmon (now Mrs. White) should have an opportunity to speak to each company. He met two of the leaders of the Boston company, Sargent and Robbins, who professed a great desire to hear Miss Harmon. Arrangements were made, and they promised to have the whole company together in Boston "the next sabbath" [Sunday] to hear her speak.

At family worship Saturday night Miss Harmon was shown in vision that there would be no meeting in Boston the next day; that the men who had expressed so strong a desire to hear her had made no appointment for her, but were going with their whole company to Randolph, and that she must go to that place, and meet both companies at the same time. It was also revealed to her that the Lord would manifest His power in their midst, and all present would have an opportunity to learn that the visions were of the Lord. Accordingly, she went early Sunday morning to Randolph, arriving [59] just as the opening hymn was being sung. Great was the astonishment of that company when Mr. and Mrs. Nichols and Miss Harmon entered the room.

In the season of prayer, at the opening of the meeting, Miss Harmon was taken off in vision, while in a kneeling posture. Sargent and Robbins arose and declared her vision to be false, and from Satan, and said that if an open Bible were laid on her breast, it would at once bring her out of the vision. Mr. Thayer, the owner of the house, placed a large quarto, ten-pound Bible open upon her chest. Immediately after the Bible was laid upon her, she arose upon her feet, and walked into the middle of the room, with the Bible open upon her left hand, and lifted as high as she could reach, with her eyes steadily looking upward, and not upon the Bible. She continued for a long time to turn over the leaves with her other hand, and place her finger upon certain passages, and correctly utter their words with a solemn voice. Many present looked at the passages where her finger pointed, to see if she spoke them correctly; for her eyes at the same time were looking upward and not toward the book. She continued thus in vision all the afternoon until almost sunset,—over six hours,—the longest vision she has ever been known to have.

In exposing the schemes of Satan against the Lord's work, this vision was in character like the one referred to above, in the days of Elisha and the king of Israel. [60]

Prophetic Delineation of Character

In the eighth chapter of Second Kings we find that the prophet "Elisha came to Damascus; and Ben-hadad the king of Syria was sick; and it was told him, saying, The man of God is come hither. And the king said unto Hazael, Take a present in thine hand, and go, meet the man of God, and inquire of the Lord by him, saying, Shall I recover of this disease? So Hazael went to meet him, and took a present with him, even of every good thing of Damascus, forty camels' burden, and came and stood before him, and said, Thy son Ben-hadad king of Syria hath sent me to thee, saying, Shall I recover of this disease? And Elisha said unto him, Go, say unto him, Thou mayest certainly recover: howbeit the Lord hath showed me that he shall surely die. [By reference to verse 15 we see that he did not die of his disease, but Hazael killed his master.] And he [Elisha] settled his countenance steadfastly, until he [Hazael] was ashamed; and the man of God wept. And Hazael said, Why weepeth my lord? And he answered, Because I know the evil that thou wilt do unto the children of Israel: their strongholds wilt thou set on fire, and their young men wilt thou slay with the sword, and wilt dash their children, and rip up their women with child. And Hazael said, But what, is thy servant a dog, that he should do this great thing? And Elisha answered, The Lord hath showed me that thou shalt be king over Syria." Verses 7-13. [61]

It seems from this record that Elisha had previously been shown in vision that Ben-hadad would be killed by one of his servants, who would then become king of Syria, and would do great evil to the children of Israel. After answering Hazael's question about his master's disease, the prophet gets a fair look at the countenance of this messenger, and, behold, he is the very one whom the Lord had shown him would be the future king of Syria.

Many are the instances witnessed by the writer, during the last fifty-eight years, in which persons previously seen in vision have come before Mrs. White, persons whom she had never met face to face until she came into a public assembly where they were. She then would single them out from the audience, by describing their person or dress, and then give a delineation of their character, manner of life, etc., more clearly than their immediate friends and acquaintances could have done. This would be accompanied with kindly reproofs for the wrong-doers, or counsel for those needing it, or words of encouragement to those battling with the trials or discouragements of life.

Attention is called, in illustration of this, to a case connected with the first visit of Mrs. White to the state of Michigan, in the spring of 1853. Neither she nor her husband had ever been west of Buffalo, New York, until the day before their first meeting in Michigan, which was held in Tyrone, Livingston County. With scarcely an exception, [62] all the believers in the state of Michigan were entire strangers to her. In this assembly she was taken off in vision, and saw all the Seventh-day Adventists in the state, then about one hundred in number. In the view given her, testimonies were borne for some present, and for others who were in the state but not at the meeting. June 2, in Jackson, Michigan, she wrote eight pages of foolscap paper, telling some of the things she had seen on this occasion. In this connection the writer is pleased to say that he has in his possession a written copy of this vision.

Among other cases described in that manuscript is the case of a woman who was trying to intrude herself among the believers. Mrs. White said the woman professed great holiness; that she had never met her, and had no knowledge of her, only what was shown to her in the Tyrone vision. This writing not only told of the woman's mode of procedure, but what she would say when reproved. Mrs. White said, "She will put on a sanctimonious look, and say, 'The Lord knows my heart.'" Mrs. White further said, "This woman is traveling about the country with a young man, while her husband, an old man [nearly twice as old as his wife], is at home, toiling with his hands to support them." She said the Lord had shown her that "notwithstanding the woman's pretension to holiness, she and the young man were guilty of violating the seventh commandment." [63]

From the Jackson meeting I was privileged to accompany Elder and Mrs. White to the other appointments of their four weeks' visit in Michigan. I was a stranger in the state, but supposed we should see the woman at some of the meetings, as the appointments were so arranged that all our people in the state could attend some one of them. With the written document in my pocket, I watched with no ordinary interest, as we went from place to place, to see how this case would develop.

Developments at Vergennes, Michigan

The appointments for the above meetings were in Jackson, Battle Creek, Bedford, Hastings, and Vergennes. The last-named place proved to be the one where the woman lived of whom Mrs. White had the view in the vision given at Tyrone. June 11 we drove forty miles to reach Vergennes. Our first meeting was to be held the next morning, two miles farther on from our lodging; and the woman described in the vision lived three miles still farther on.

At eleven o'clock, June 12, our meeting was opened. Mrs. White sat at the left end of the rostrum; I sat next to her; Elder M. E. Cornell sat next to me; and Elder White was at the right of the rostrum, speaking. After he had talked about fifteen minutes, an old man and a young man came in together, and sat down on the front seat, next to the rostrum. They were accompanied by a tall, slim, dark-complexioned woman, who took her seat [64] near the door. As these persons came in, Mrs. White looked at them steadily for a minute or two, then raised her fan, and in a low whisper asked the writer if he noticed the persons who just came in. Said she: "Those are the ones the vision is about. When my husband closes his discourse, I will relate the vision, and you will see whether they are the ones."

After a short discourse from Elder White, Mrs. White arose, and quoted the text, "Be ye clean that bear the vessels of the Lord." She said it is not the Lord's order to call a woman to travel about the country with any other man than her husband. Finally she said plainly: "That woman who sat down a short time ago near the door, claims that God has called her to preach. She is traveling with this young man who just sat down in front of the desk, while this old man—her husband, God pity him!—is toiling at home to earn money, which they are using to carry on their iniquity. She professes to be very holy—to be sanctified—but with all her pretensions to holiness, God has shown me that she and this young man are guilty of violating the seventh commandment."

As Mrs. White bore her testimony, there was an anxious looking toward Mrs. —, the woman reproved, to see how she received it, and what she would say. Had she been innocent of the charge against her, it would naturally be expected of her to rise up and deny the whole thing. If guilty, and [65] grossly corrupt, she might be none too good to deny it all, even though she knew it to be true. Instead of this, she did just what the testimony said she would do when reproved: she slowly rose to her feet, while every eye in the house was fixed upon her, and, putting on a sanctimonious look, said, "The Lord knows my heart," and sat down without saying another word. She had said just what the written testimony said she would say, and said it in the same manner. In the practical working of the gift of prophecy this case compares, in kind, with that of Hazael before Elisha.

We have now made a comparison of Mrs. White's visions with *fifteen* points mentioned in the Bible respecting the visions of God's prophets and their practical working, and conclude that as "the spirits of the prophets are subject to the prophets," and as "like causes produce like results," the results manifested in this case are a substantial proof that these visions are from the Spirit of the Lord, and are a token of the Lord's care for the remnant church, which He is gathering out of the world in these last days.

RULES FOR DISCERNING TRUE PROPHETS

The prophet Isaiah, in speaking of the situation of affairs existing in the last days, says: "Bind up the testimony, seal the law among My disciples. And I will wait upon the Lord, that hideth His face from the house of Jacob, and I will look for Him... And when they shall say unto you, [66] Seek unto them that have familiar spirits, and unto wizards that peep, and that mutter: should not a people seek unto their God? for the living to the dead? To the law and to the testimony: if they speak not according to this word, it is because there is no light in them." Isaiah 8:16-20.

In this scripture attention is called to a people engaged in restoring the seal to God's law—a people who are waiting upon the Lord, engaged in His service. They are looking for Him; that is, they are looking for His coming—this, too, in a time when spirits, professing to be spirits of the dead, are asking the people to seek to them. Some heed that call, and seek to the dead for knowledge; but the Lord invites His people to seek to Him. That is virtually saying that if they seek to Him He will give them special instruction. They need not seek to the dead, who can give them no information; for "neither have they any more a portion forever in anything that is done under the sun;" and "the dead know not anything." Ecclesiastes 9:6, 5.

Rule One

In the above scripture a rule is given by which all communications are to be tested: "If they speak not according to this word, it is because there is no light in them." All communications from the Lord will speak in harmony with His word and His law. [67]

Applying this rule to the writings of Mrs. White, I would say that during the last fifty-eight years I have carefully read her testimonies, comparing them with the law of God and the testimony of the Bible, and I find perfect harmony between the two. Her instructions do not come in to give any new revelation to take the place of the Scripture, but rather to show where and how, in these times, people are liable to be led astray, to be led from the Word. The position that the testimonies of Mrs. White occupy can be best told in what she herself has written respecting them:

"The word of God is sufficient to enlighten the most beclouded mind, and may be understood by those who have any desire to understand it. But, notwithstanding all this, some who profess to make the word of God their study, are found living in direct opposition to its plainest teachings. Then, to leave men and women without excuse, God gives plain and pointed testimonies, bringing them back to the Word that they have neglected to follow... Additional truth is not brought out; but God has through the testimonies simplified the great truths already given, and in His own chosen way brought them before the people, to awaken and impress the mind with them, that all may be left without excuse... The testimonies are not to belittle the word of God, but to exalt it, and attract minds to it, that the beautiful simplicity of truth may impress all."—Testimonies for the Church 5:663, 665. [68]

Rule Two — True Prophets

By looking at the testimony of the apostle John, we find another rule describing the teaching of true prophets. He says:

> "Beloved, believe not every spirit, but try the spirits whether they are of God: because many false prophets are gone out into the world. Hereby know ye the Spirit of God: Every spirit that confesseth that Jesus Christ

is come in the flesh is of God: and every spirit that confesseth not that Jesus Christ is come in the flesh is not of God: and this is that spirit of antichrist, whereof ye have heard that it should come; and even now already is it in the world." 1 John 4:1-3.

Note carefully the foregoing scripture. It does not say whosoever confesses that Jesus Christ "did come in the flesh," but, "IS COME IN THE FLESH;" that is, that He comes, by His Spirit, and dwells IN US, in response to our faith. This, in fact, is the central truth of the gospel, "Christ in you, the hope of glory." Ephesians 3:17; Colossians 1:27.

The practical theme found in all of Mrs. White's writings is the necessity of an indwelling Saviour if we would make any advancement in the heavenly way. Her writings teach the necessity of Christ first, last, and all the time. As an illustration of this fact, attention is called to her book, "Steps to Christ," of which more than one hundred thousand copies have been sold in English, to say nothing [69] of the thousands of copies in more than twenty foreign languages in which it is now printed.

Rule Three — False Prophets

John gives a rule for detecting false prophets, which we designate as rule three. Speaking of false prophets, the apostle says, "They are of the world: therefore speak they of the world, and the world heareth them." 1 John 4:5. This shows that the teaching of false prophets will pander to the carnal heart, instead of exalting the self-denying and cross-bearing way. False prophets will teach "smooth things," instead of exalting "the Holy One of Israel." Isaiah 30:10, 11. Any one who reads even a few pages of Mrs. White's writings, can see that they are in the direct line of self-denial and cross-bearing, not of a nature to please a worldly, carnal heart. See 1 John 2:10.

Rule Four

In tracing this subject still further, we will take, as a fourth rule, the words of the apostle James: "Take, my brethren, the prophets, who have spoken in the name of the Lord, for an example of suffering affliction, and of patience." James 5:10. When we read the experience of those ancient prophets, we learn that one of their greatest trials was to see Israel reject, or go contrary to, the plain testimony borne to them. A brief study of those times will show at once the character of both true and false prophets. "Thus saith the Lord of Hosts, Harken not unto the words of the [70] prophets that prophesy unto you: they make you vain: they speak a vision of their own heart, and not out of the mouth of the Lord." Jeremiah 23:16.

There is nothing in the writings of Mrs. White to make the reader vain; but, as expressed by another: "I have received great spiritual benefit times without number from the testimonies. Indeed, I never read them without feeling reproof for my lack of faith in God, lack of devotion, and lack of earnestness in saving souls." Surely, then, the effect of Mrs. White's testimonies is vastly different from that of the teachings of false prophets, as described by Jeremiah.

The prophet tells us also how the false prophets will teach: "They say still unto them that despise Me, The Lord hath said, Ye shall have peace; and they say unto every one that walketh after the imagination of his own heart, No evil shall come upon you." Verse 17.

As to the nature of Mrs. White's teachings in her testimonies, I will quote the following words from a careful reader: "I find the most earnest appeals to obey God, to love Jesus, to believe the Scriptures, and to search them constantly. Such nearness to God, such earnest devotion, such solemn appeals to live a holy life, can only be prompted by the Spirit of God."

True and False Prophets Compared

When considering the character of the Lord's prophets in ancient times, the trait of faithfulness [71] in reproving sins, even when surrounded by a vastly superior number of false prophets, is particularly noticeable. Their testimony is not withheld from the highest in authority; even kings were not exempt from reproof, as is seen in the case of Elijah before Ahab.

Because of Israel's departure from the true worship of God, the Lord brought famine upon the land. In response to Elijah's petition, rain for the space of three years and six months had been withheld. Then the Lord said to Elijah, "Go, show thyself unto Ahab; and I will send rain upon the earth. And Elijah went to show himself unto Ahab." "And it came to pass, when Ahab saw Elijah, that Ahab said unto him, Art thou he that troubleth Israel? And he answered, I have not troubled Israel; but thou, and thy father's house, in that ye have forsaken the commandments of the Lord, and thou hast followed Baalim." 1 Kings 18:1, 2, 17, 18.

Often has the writer heard Mrs. White advise persons as to what they would do, and they would protest that they *never* would do it. She would say, "If you do it not, the Lord has not spoken by me." Notwithstanding their protest, they did, at last, the thing they had solemnly declared they would *never* do.

RULE FIVE — TRUE PROPHECIES ARE FULFILLED

There is a statement made by Moses relative to the true and the false prophets, found in the eighteenth [72] chapter of Deuteronomy, which, in our consideration of rules for discerning true and false prophets, may be designated as rule *five*. He says: "And if thou say in thine heart, How shall we know the word which the Lord hath not spoken? when a prophet speaketh in the name of the Lord, if the thing follow not, nor come to pass, that is the thing which the Lord hath not spoken, but the prophet hath spoken it presumptuously: thou shalt not be afraid of him." Verses 21, 22.

The same thing is also found in the following scriptures: "Who is he that saith, and it cometh to pass, when the Lord commandeth it not?" Lamentations 3:37. Of the prophet Samuel it was said, "All that he saith cometh surely to pass." 1 Samuel 9:6. "When the word of the prophet shall come to pass, then shall the prophet be known, that the Lord hath truly sent him." Jeremiah 28:9.

It is now over fifty-eight years since the writer first saw Mrs. E. G. White in prophetic vision. During these years many prophetic statements have been made by her relative to things that would take place. Some of these predictions relate to events already fulfilled, and some are in process of fulfilment, while others are still future. As to those relating to the past or present events, I know not of a single instance of failure. Before noting some of the predictions made during these fifty-eight years, it may be well to note some that were made previously, which were in print in 1852. [73]

Before me lies a book published by Joseph Bates, in January, 1849, entitled "A Seal of the Living God." In the book is an account of a vision given to Mrs. White in the home of Otis Nichols, Dorchester, Massachusetts, on the evening of November 18, 1848. At that time there was a condition of war, rioting, and confusion, which began on the twenty-second of February of that year, in the city of Paris, France, and had spread to over thirty of the principalities, states, and governments of Europe. Modern Spiritualism began its "rappings" at Hydesville, New York, about the same time that the stir among the nations began. The first-day Adventists claimed that this stir among the nations was the rally to the battle of the great day of the Lord, and that the "rapping spirits" were the spirits of devils, going forth to gather the nations, as predicted in Revelation 16:14, and that the Lord was immediately coming.

At that time the few who had begun to observe the seventh-day Sabbath had just discovered, from the seventh chapter of the book of Revelation, a "sealing message," which must go forth to prepare a people to stand in the great day of the Lord. These few said, "The last great battle can not come yet; for here is a sealing work to prepare a people to stand in that great day." Mr. and Mrs. White and Mr. Bates were the three public laborers who were then teaching the Sabbath truth and the "sealing message." They, with the few who had already [74] accepted the message, were among the very poor of the world.

On the evening already mentioned, these laborers and other brethren met at Otis Nichols's home, to pray the Lord to guide them in publishing the "sealing message" to the world. As they prayed, Mrs. White was taken off in vision. While in vision, she said of the Sabbath truth: "It is the seal! That truth arises, and is on the increase, *stronger* and *stronger*. It is coming up! It arises, commencing from the rising of the sun. Like the sun, at first cold, it grows warmer and sends its rays. The angels are holding the four winds. It is God that restrains the powers. The angels have *not* let go; for the saints are not all sealed. When Michael stands up, this trouble will be all over the earth. They [the winds of war, etc.] are just ready to blow. There is a check put on because the saints are not sealed. Yea, publish the things thou hast seen and heard, and the blessing of God will attend."

At the time that vision was given, it did really look as if the nations of the world would soon be in a "whirlwind" of war. Of the situation, United States Senator Choate said, "It has seemed to me as if the prerogatives of crowns, and the rights of men, and the hoarded-up resentments of a thousand years, were about to unsheathe the sword for a conflict in which blood shall flow, as in apocalyptic vision, 'to the bridles of the horses.'" [75]

In a few months the nations were all quiet again; but this change came on so unexpectedly that Horace Greeley, in speaking of it in the New York *Tribune*, said, "It was a great wonder to politicians what started all that turmoil of the nations, but a greater wonder still *what* stopped it all so suddenly."

After coming out of the vision already spoken of, Mrs. White said to her husband: "I saw that you must begin to print a paper, small at first; but as you send it out to the people, they will read it, and will send you money with which to print it. It will be a success from the first. From that small beginning it [the publishing work] was shown to me as streams of light that went around the entire world."

The few believers had faith in that prediction, but were without money to begin the work. Many prayers were offered to God to open the way. In June, 1849, the way opened, Mr. White having opportunity to mow forty acres of grass with a handscythe. With the money thus obtained, in July, 1849, he printed the first number of a small paper entitled *Present Truth*. During 1849-50 eleven numbers of this paper were printed. In No.5 we read this statement, which was written by Mr. White: "The money our readers have sent in has been more than enough to print the paper. With the remainder we have met the expenses of Mrs. White and myself as we went from place to place [76] to hold meetings." So it was a "success from the first."

How from that "small beginning" has the published truth "gone around the world"! At the present time Seventh-day Adventists have twenty-seven publishing houses in different parts of the world. In these houses over seventy steam-power presses are used. This truth is issued from these offices in sixty-seven languages of the world. The literature of the denomination in these languages consists of over 2,700 different books, pamphlets, and tracts, and 126 periodicals, either weekly, monthly, or quarterly. Each one of the smallest papers is about the size of the first paper, *Present Truth*. Up to January, 1911, over eleven million dollars' worth of the books had been sold. Publishing houses, sanitariums, schools, and missions are established twice around the world-both north and south of the equator. That prediction which looked "preposterous" to our opponents in 1848, is surely in a well-advanced state of fulfilment in 1911.

TRUE PROPHECIES

We will now notice predictions made by Mrs. White concerning modern Spiritualism, in the years 1849-50.

That of the former date reads: "I saw that the mysterious knocking in New York and other places was the power of Satan, and that such things would be more and more common, clothed in a religious garb so as to lull the deceived to greater security, [77] and to draw the minds of God's people, if possible, to those things, and cause them to doubt the teachings and power of the Holy Ghost."—Early Writings, 43.

At the time of this vision there was only the "rapping" manifestation. Questions were asked, and the answer of "yes" or "no" was given by either two or three "raps." The greater part of the people regarded the "rappings," as they were then called, as trickery, or sleight-of-hand performance. At that time the idea was not even suggested that "spirit rappings" would assume to be a religious organization, as it has since done, with its titles of "Rev. —, pastor of the First Spiritualist Church of —," etc.

In the vision of August 24, 1850, we read: "I was shown that by the rapping and mesmerism, these modern magicians would yet account for all the miracles wrought by our Lord Jesus Christ, and that many would believe that all the mighty works of the Son of God when on the earth were accomplished by this same power."

It is since that vision was given in 1850 that Spiritualists have taught, both in their oral instructions and in their printed books and papers (what they did not teach previously to that date), that all the miracles of

Christ were wrought by the power of mesmerism, and that He was only a "well-developed medium."

Another statement is given, taken from "Early [78] Writings," page 87, first printed in 1853: "I saw the rapping delusion—what progress it was making, and that if it were possible, it would deceive the very elect. Satan will have power to bring before us the *appearance* of forms purporting to be our relatives or friends now sleeping in Jesus. It will be made to appear as if these friends were present; the words that they uttered while here, with which we were familiar, will be spoken, and the same tone of voice that they had while living will fall upon the ear. All this is to deceive the saints, and to ensnare them into the belief of this delusion."

At the time this vision was given, the mode of communicating with the spirits was by calling over the letters of the alphabet, and spelling out the communication, and by a "rap" the spirits designated the letter wanted. No one had, at that date, heard of a case of what has been so much talked of during the last thirty years,—the *"materializing of spirits;"* that is, the spirit assuming a bodily form, shaking hands with people, and talking with them in tones that they claim to recognize as the exact tone of voice of a dead relative or friend.

It was about the years 1857-58,—four years after Mrs. White had put in print that the spirits would assume the forms of dead friends,—that mediums claimed to see their friends and to hear them speak.

In the light of this rule for testing prophets, what can we say of the predictions made through [79] Mrs. White concerning Spiritualism? She stated, when it was not here, what would be done. The thing predicted came. That is, according to the Bible, proof of divine inspiration in the vision.

VISION OF THE CIVIL WAR

In the further study of this question we refer to a prediction made in a vision by Mrs. White, at Parkville, Michigan, January 12, 1861, concerning the Civil War that was to come in the United States. At that time only one state, South Carolina, had passed a secession ordinance.[1] The people in the

---

[1] South Carolina passed its ordinance December 20, 1860.

North little thought of a war growing out of that. In the New York *Tribune* of that week, Horace Greeley, the editor, said, "A few old women with broomsticks could go down there and beat out all the rebellion there is in South Carolina." In speaking of it the week before, he said: "If some one with the firmness of Andrew Jackson should go down there and say, 'South Carolina, where are you going?' they would reply, 'Back into the Union again, sir.'"

After Mrs. White came out of the vision already referred to, she arose before the congregation, and said: "There is not a person in this house that has even dreamed of the trouble that is coming upon this land. People are making light of the secession ordinance of South Carolina [some of the leading men of Parkville, while she thus spoke, sneered at the ideas she was advancing], but I have just been [80] shown that a large number of states will join that state, and there will be a most terrible war. In this vision I have seen large armies of both sides gathered on the field of battle. I heard the booming of the cannon, and saw the dead and dying on every hand. I saw the field after the battle, all covered with the dead and dying. Then I was carried to prisons, and saw the sufferings of those in want who were wasting away," etc. She further stated, "There are men in this house who will lose sons in that war." [2]

This vision, when given, was directly contrary to all Northern sentiment, but was nevertheless accurately fulfilled. Before the month of May, 1861, eleven states had seceded, and elected their Confederate president. On the twelfth of April the first gun of the war was fired on Fort Sumter, which surrendered on the thirteenth. The Northern idea of the war was then so meager that even President Lincoln called for only seventy-five thousand men for three months, to put down the rebellion. Little did the people in responsible places think they were entering upon a war to continue to the spring of 1865,—a war in which the North would have in the field 2,859,132 men, and the South probably half that number.

Not only was this vision accurately fulfilled concerning the secession of the states and the war [81] itself,, but as the war continued, other things were predicted. At first the war was conducted with the thought of pre-

---

[2] There were at least *ten* men in that house that day who lost sons in the war, and among them the very fathers who sneered when the vision was related.

serving the Union, allowing slavery to remain; but while that was the case, the North met many sad reverses. As I heard expressed by Governor St. John, of Kansas, "Had we whipped the rebels, the politicians would have patched up a peace, and the Union would have then continued with slavery, and we would have it to-day."[3]

As the Northern army met these reverses, national *fast*-days were appointed, and all Christians were to plead with the Lord to manifest His power in bringing the war to a close. In a vision given to Mrs. White January 4, 1862, speaking of these fasts, she said: "And yet a national fast is proclaimed! Saith the Lord, 'Is not this the fast that I have chosen? to loose the bands of wickedness, to undo the heavy burdens, and to let the oppressed go free, and that ye break every yoke?' When our nation observes the fast which God hath chosen, then will He accept their prayers as far as the war is concerned; but now they enter not into His ear."

Five months after this vision, the politicians of the North began to call for desperate measures. In June, 1862, the *Republican Standard*, of New Bedford, Massachusetts, said, "It is time to put into vigorous exercise that severity which is the truest mercy; it is time to proclaim freedom to the slave, and thus strike treason to the heart." [82]

On January 1, 1863, President Lincoln issued his Emancipation Proclamation. Of it Governor St. John, in the speech previously mentioned, said, "But after Lincoln issued his famous Emancipation Proclamation, we had swung round on God's side, and could not lose." From that time it was a course of almost continuous success that attended the Northern army.

Of the predictions through Mrs. White concerning the war, we can truly say, "All this came;" and can we not, with firmer faith than exhibited by *the queen of Babylon*, truly say that it was the Spirit of God that taught these things? Daniel 5:10-12.

The Lord's revelation of what He would do was through His servants the prophets ("Surely the Lord God will do nothing, but He revealeth His secret unto His servants the prophets." Amos 3:7); and when the thing predicted came to pass, He expected all who professed to be His people to acknowledge it as a proof that He spoke the word, and that the instrument

---

[3] Speech in Ottawa, Illinois, June 29, 1891.

through whom He spoke was one of His true prophets. This principle is just as true in these modern days as in ancient times, and should be kept in mind when studying the instruction given by Paul, in 1 Thessalonians 5:21, to "prove all things" that come in the form of prophesyings."

Messenger Party

As a further application of the above rule, we call attention to a prediction made by Mrs. White [83] in a vision given in Oswego, New York, June 20, 1855. It related to what was then called "The Messenger Party," which consisted of disaffected ones, who, having left the ranks, began a united opposition to the visions, claiming that, when rid of them, the third angel's message would at once "go with a loud cry." This party printed a paper called the *Messenger of Truth*. From this the party was named. They claimed to have more preachers than were left with us, and tauntingly said to Seventh-day Adventist ministers, "We will follow up and get all your converts." One by the name of Drew put it in these words: "You go ahead and shake the bush, and we will follow up and catch *all* the birds." The conflict was fierce, and the opposition bitter. As expressed of them by another, "There is nothing to which they will not stoop; and they are never likely to be out of scandal with which to assail those who have incurred their displeasure."

Until the Lord spoke directly concerning this party, our leading ministers considered it their duty to answer the scandalous falsehoods that were published in the *Messenger of Truth*. Elders White, Waggoner, Cornell, and Frisbie, and the writer, counseled together, and had arranged to write a reply to the malicious fabrications, each taking a separate line of attack. Just at this time the vision (the writer being present) was given in Oswego. [84]

After coming out of the vision, Mrs. White, speaking to Elder White and the writer, said: "Brethren, you are mistaken as to your duty to answer the slanderous writings of the *Messenger*. It is only a trick of the enemy to divert you from using your time in spreading the truth. When you answer *one* of their lies, they will manufacture *two* more. The Lord says to let them alone, and go on with your work as if there was no such people on the earth, and in less than six weeks they will be at war among themselves. The candid ones will see their error and come back. The *Messenger* company will go to pieces, and their paper go down, while the third angel's message will advance more rapidly than ever. When their paper goes down, you will find that our ranks have doubled."

And "SO IT WAS." We let them alone, and made no reference to them or their work in the *Review*. First they complained, then they growled, and dared us for battle. In less than four weeks some of their financial supporters left them, and the dissension and fight were on among themselves. The cause of present truth advanced in every phase of its work. A statement made in the *Review*, January 14, 1858, just after the *Messenger* paper "breathed its last," having had a sickly existence of about three years, shows how accurately the prediction made in the Oswego vision was fulfilled. Speaking of the result of the *Messenger* work, the editor said: "At the time of the disaffection, when [85] the effort was made to break down the *Review*, the church property at the office was worth only seven hundred dollars. Since it has increased to five thousand. Then there were about one thousand paying subscribers; now there are two thousand, besides quite a *free* list." As the number of paying subscribers to the *Review* had exactly doubled, so the number of believers had increased more than twofold.

"BE IN HEALTH"

John, the beloved apostle, wrote to Gaius these words: "I wish above all things that thou mayest prosper and be in health, even as thy soul prospereth." 3 John 1:2. This thought is also expressed in Paul's prayer for the people of God, even down to this time: "And the very God of peace sanctify you wholly; and I pray God your whole spirit and soul and body [life, mind, and body] be preserved blameless unto the coming of our Lord Jesus Christ. Faithful is He that calleth you, who also will do it." 1 Thessalonians 5:23, 24.

Instead of a spurious sanctification, the Lord delights in a truly sanctified people; but to perfect them and to accomplish His work in them, He *hews* them by the prophets. Hosea 6:5. This fact understood leads to inquiry concerning what the Lord is now doing through the gift of prophecy in teaching a sanctification that corrects those wrong habits of eating and drinking which tend to build up the carnal nature, instead of mortifying our members. Colossians 3:5. [86]

OTSEGO VISION

June 6, 1863, at Otsego, Michigan, Mrs. White had the great and wonderful vision on healthful living,—disease and its causes, drugs and their evil effects, etc. Regarding the nature of the principles there taught, and the proofs in the vision itself of its divine inspiration, I will quote from the words of Dr. J. H. Kellogg, in the preface to the book called *"Christian Temperance and Bible Hygiene,"* published in 1890:

> "1. At the time the writings referred to first appeared, the subject of health was almost wholly ignored, not only by the people to whom they were addressed, but by the world at large.
>
> "2. The few advocating the necessity of a reform in physical habits, propagated, in connection with the advocacy of genuine reformatory principles, the most patent and in some instances disgusting errors.
>
> "3. Nowhere, and by no one, was there presented a systematic and harmonious body of hygienic truths, free from patent errors, and consistent with the Bible and the principles of the Christian religion.
>
> "Under these circumstances, the writings referred to made their appearance. The principles taught were not enforced by scientific authority, but were presented in a simple, straightforward manner by one who makes no pretense to scientific knowledge, but claims to write by the aid and authority of divine enlightenment. [87]
>
> "How have the principles presented under such peculiar circumstances and with such remarkable claims stood the test of time and experience? is a question which may very properly be asked. Its answer is to be found in facts which are capable of the amplest verification... The principles which a quarter of a century ago [now more than forty-seven years ago] were either entirely ignored or made the butt of ridicule, have quietly won their way into public confidence and esteem, until the world has quite forgotten that they have not always been thus accepted... Every one of the principles

advanced more than a quarter of a century ago is fortified in the strongest possible manner by scientific evidence...

"It certainly must be regarded as a thing remarkable, and evincing UNMISTAKABLE EVIDENCE OF DIVINE INSIGHT AND DIRECTION, that in the midst of confused and conflicting teachings, claiming the authority of science... a person making no claims to scientific knowledge or erudition should have been able to organize ... a body of hygienic principles so harmonious, so consistent, and so genuine that the discussions, and researches, and discoveries, and the experience of a quarter of a century, have not resulted in the overthrow of a single principle, but have only served to establish the doctrines taught."

Since 1863, the time when the diet question and healthful living were unfolded to Mrs. White, the [88] subject of health reform has been classed with the preparatory work for fitting up a people to meet the events before us. The Lord is leading His people "back, step by step, to His original design,—that man should subsist upon the natural products of the earth."

Mrs. White, in 1863, further stated that from what had been revealed to her, "the animals whose flesh was used for food would become more and more diseased, until finally it would be unsafe to eat their flesh. The Lord was in mercy introducing these principles to His people, that by practicing them they might be better fitted to meet and resist the increase of disease upon the human family, and stand unharmed amid the seven last plagues." The present increase of disease in the domestic animals is startling the nations of the earth. The Lord's people see in this fact the fulfilling of the predictions made forty-seven years ago concerning this very thing.

Predictions Concerning Sunday Laws

In "Testimonies," volume 5, page 451, printed in 1885, is a statement as to *how* Sunday laws would be passed in the United States. It reads: "To secure popularity and patronage, legislators will yield to the *demand* for a Sunday law."

Now, let us see how this has already been done. In 1892 a *demand* was made of Congress to prohibit the opening on Sunday of the world's fair, which was to be in Chicago, Illinois, from May to [89] October of that year. Such a law was passed July 19, 1892, under just such a pressure as above predicted. And be it remembered that this is the *first* time that the United States Congress ever legislated on the Sabbath question.

The churches sent in immense lists of names, and petitions, and telegrams, not only petitioning Congress, but kindly (?) informing the congressmen "that we do hereby pledge ourselves and each other, that we will, from this time henceforth, refuse to vote for or support for any office or position of trust, any member of Congress, either senator or representative, who shall vote for any further aid of any kind for the world's fair except on conditions named in these resolutions." The conditions were that the fair should be closed on Sunday.

As a sample of the talk on the floors of Congress, when the bill was passed, read the following: "I should like to see the disclaimer put in white and black and proposed by the Congress of the United States. Write it. How would you write it? ... Word it, if you dare; advocate it, if you dare; *how many who voted for it would ever come back here again?*—None, I hope. You endanger yourselves by opposing it." Thus we see how that testimony, given in 1885, has *been* and is *being* fulfilled.

Catholic and Protestant Unity

Here is another prediction found also in Testimonies for the Church 5:207, 1885: "When Protestantism [90] shall stretch her hand across the gulf to grasp the hand of the Roman power, when she shall reach over the abyss to clasp hands with Spiritualism, when, under the influence of this threefold union, our country shall repudiate every principle of its constitution as a Protestant and republican government, and shall make provision for the propagation of papal falsehoods and delusions, then we may know that the time has come for the marvelous working of Satan, and that the end is near."

To show how the first part of this prediction is already fulfilling we need only to call attention to what is transpiring around us. See Protestants, both ministers and people, courting the favor of Catholics, inviting them to attend their associations and join with them in their religious and political federations. Be it remembered that hardly a vestige of what is now seen in this line was apparent in 1885, when the above testimony was given.

As a sample of how the Protestants are reaching for the hand and help of papists, I will quote from the Kansas City (Missouri) *Star* of March 18, 1896.

CATHOLIC AND METHODIST ST. PATRICK'S DAY

A speech was delivered in Coate's Opera House, Kansas City, Missouri, on St. Patrick's day, March 17, 1896, by Dr. Mitchell, pastor of the leading Methodist Church of Kansas City. The *Star* speaks of a portion of the speech as "a dramatic little [91] scene."." Dr. Mitchell was loudly applauded when he said this: "Bigotry is the child of ignorance. We are bigoted because we do not know our neighbors well enough. We Protestants have been taught to believe unutterable things of Catholics. Catholics have been taught to believe unutterable things of Protestants. Now we discover our mistaken notions of each other when we get close enough to look into each other's eyes and clasp each other's hands; if we only knew each other more we would love each other better. We have stood apart and criticized. Shame upon the followers of the blessed Christ! All Christians have been redeemed by the same precious blood; we are sustained by the same divine grace, and expect to reach the same heaven. Say, brothers, we had better be getting acquainted with each other down here."

Dr. Mitchell then turned to Father Dalton (Catholic priest), who sat just behind him, and, reaching out his hand, said, "Here, Brother Dalton, is my hand." Father Dalton arose and clasped the extended hand, and as Dr. Mitchell shook it, he said: "It would be an awful shame if, after living so long in the same city on earth, we would have to get an angel to introduce us to each other in heaven. Let us get acquainted here on earth." The audience applauded, and after Father Dalton sat down, Dr. Mitchell continued his speech. Let it be remembered that that audience was largely Protestant which joined in that vociferous cheering that followed this speech. [92]

The Church Federation of Protestant Churches, in 1905, sent to Cardinal Gibbons (Catholic) the ten points of their plan of operations. He replied that he "fully approved of their plans."

PREDICTION OF SANITARIUM SITES

On March 18, 1902, a number of us were called together at the Los Angeles treatment rooms, on Third Street, to consider a proposition to buy a site on the corner of South Hill and Fourth Streets for a sanitarium. The price was $100,000 for the bare lot, and this money would have to be hired, as also the money to erect a sanitarium, if one was built. As there was much hesitancy with us on the propriety of making such a venture, a testimony from Sister White was received through the mail. She was five hundred miles off, and knew not of our council on any such proposition. The testimony said: "Do not build a sanitarium in Los Angeles. Our sanitariums should be out in the country. While it may be right to hire treatment rooms in the city, do not build in the city. The Lord has shown me that there are properties that have been erected that are just fitted to our work, which for some cause have not been occupied, that will be offered to us at very low figures." That settled the question with us.

No one of our people knew of any such properties. Search has resulted in what? Glendale, Paradise Valley, and Loma Linda, which were all fitted ready for our work, and each obtained at about one third of what had been invested in them. [93]

These predictions made through Mrs. White, so accurately fulfilled and fulfilling, in accordance with rule *five*, show her to be a true prophet of the Lord.

Rule Six — Miracles Not a Test of a True Prophet

It has been affirmed by many theological writers, and stated in commentaries on the Scriptures, that the sign of a true prophet is the working of miracles.

If the working of miracles is proof of a true prophet, then the "false prophet" mentioned in Revelation 19:20 would be declared after all a true prophet; for it is said, "The beast was taken, and with him the false prophet that wrought miracles before him, with which he deceived them that had received the mark of the beast." The same power is mentioned again in Revelation 13:14, as deceiving "them that dwell on the earth by the means of those miracles which he had power to do in the sight of the beast." By the same application of this rule, we would be driven to the conclusion that even Satan is a true prophet. Certain spirits that will do a special work under the sixth of the seven last plagues, are called "the spirits of devils, working miracles, which go forth unto the kings of the earth and of the whole world, to gather them to the battle of that great day of God Almighty." Revelation 16:14.

It is true that miracles are recorded as being wrought by some of the prophets, as in the case of Elijah, Elisha, and Paul. But who has found [94] any record in the Bible of the miracles of Isaiah, Jeremiah, Daniel, Hosea, Joel, Amos, etc.? Yet these were true prophets of the Lord, and are shown to be such by the rules the Lord has given to test true prophets.

That the working of miracles is not the test of a true prophet, is clearly seen by reading the Scripture record of John the Baptist. That he was a prophet is shown by the prediction of his father, Zacharias, in relating the vision God had given him respecting the son that should be born to him: "And thou, child, shalt be called the prophet of the Highest: for thou shalt go before the face of the Lord to prepare His ways." Luke 1:76. Our Saviour Himself recognized John as that very prophet who should prepare the way before Him; for of John He said: "But what went ye out for to see? A prophet? Yea, I say unto you, and much more than a prophet. This is he, of whom it is written, Behold, I send My messenger before Thy face, which shall prepare Thy way before Thee. For I say unto you, Among those that are born of women there is not a greater prophet than John the Baptist." Luke 7:26-28.

Here then is a plain statement of the Saviour that John was a prophet. Let us apply the test of miracle-working, and see the result. In the Gospel as written by John the evangelist, we have these words: "And many resorted unto Him [Christ], and said, John did no miracle: but all things that [95] John spake of this Man were true." John 10:41. This statement alone is a complete refutation of the claim that the sign of a true prophet is the working of miracles.

This sixth rule teaches that if a miracle is wrought by a pretender, there will be seen with it, when carefully tested, a departure from the sacred truths of God's word, and a lowering of the standard, to meet a heart inclined to shun the way of self-denial. The Lord permits such pretender to arise, and his course is a test to the true child of God, giving him an opportunity to weigh carefully the tendency or motive of said miracle-worker. Those who cling to God's word, instead of being captivated by the false miracle-worker, come forth strong in God as the result of such experience.

In these evil days when many are claiming to be "faith healers," "divine healers," or "Christian Science healers," etc., it would be well to apply closely the Scriptural rules; for it will need divine rules, and the illumination of the Holy Spirit, to enable us clearly to discern the intent and purpose of some of these "healers," so subtle in their work; while on the other hand are those who openly disregard God's law and His truth for this time.

In this rule six we are counseled to watch the nature of the testimony, whether it draws us nearer to the Lord, or away from Him. Virtually, we are counseled to test the prophet by all the rules, [96] and not decide that he is a true prophet because apparently he is in harmony with one rule. I say apparently, for if perchance he made a prediction, the next question naturally arises, Where did he get his prediction of events to take place? We understand from the Scriptures that anciently unprincipled men, false prophets, "stole" the words of true prophets, and passed them off as their prophecy, seeking thus to succeed in their deception.

The Lord has told His people in these times that "the devil is a careful student of the prophecies of the Bible." And why is this? Is it to learn the truth, that he may help on the work of the Lord?—No, by no means, but rather that he may tell some of these things that are coming-having stolen them from the Lord's prophets—thus making it appear that his prophets are true ones.

"Satan closely watches events, and when he finds one who has a specially strong spirit of opposition to the truth of God, he will even reveal to him unfulfilled events, that he may more firmly secure himself a seat in his heart... During his experience of nearly six thousand years he has lost none of his skill and shrewdness. All this time he has been a close observer of all that concerns our race."—Testimonies for the Church 2:171, 172.

Although Satan's prophets may do miracles, or may speak of things to come, by the aid of what they have seen take place (as the death of a person [97] occurring at a certain hour), or tell of an event to come (of which they "stole" their knowledge from God's prophet), yet in applying all the rules to their case, it will soon be seen where they fail to be in harmony with the Lord's standard of true prophets. Satan will not teach submission to God's law, but rather the service of other gods, even though it be the self-pleasing way of shunning the path of self-denial.

RULE SEVEN — "BY THEIR FRUITS YE SHALL KNOW THEM"

"Beware of false prophets, which come to you in sheep's clothing, but inwardly they are ravening wolves. Ye shall know them by their fruits. Do men gather grapes of thorns, or figs of thistles? Even so every good tree bringeth forth good fruit, but a corrupt tree bringeth forth evil fruit. A good tree can not bring forth evil fruit, neither can a corrupt tree bring forth good fruit. Every tree that bringeth not forth good fruit is hewn down, and cast into the fire. Wherefore by their fruits ye shall know them." Matthew 7:15-20.

These words of our Saviour recognize the fact that the gift of prophecy would exist in the gospel age. If no true prophets were to be connected with the work, and every prophetic manifestation was to be from an evil source, would He not have said, "Beware of prophets"? The fact that He tells us so definitely how each kind may be known, is the best of evidence that in the work of the Comforter, [98] the Holy Spirit, is showing "things to come" (John 16:13), would be the true gift of prophecy. This rule, which in our enumeration we have called rule seven, is an infallible one. Christ did not say, "Ye may know them by their fruits," but, positively, "Ye shall know them by their fruits."

We inquire, What is the fruit to be seen in the work of genuine gifts of the Spirit of God? The answer is found in the statement of Paul respecting the purpose of the Lord in placing the gifts in the church: "Wherefore He saith, When He ascended up on high, He led captivity captive, and gave gifts unto men... And He gave some, apostles; and some, prophets; and some, evangelists; and some, pastors and teachers; for the perfecting of the saints, for the work of the ministry, for the edifying of the body of Christ: till we all come in the unity ["into the unity," margin] of the faith, and of the knowledge of the Son of God, unto a perfect man, unto the measure of the stature of the fullness of Christ: that we henceforth be no more children, tossed to and fro, and carried about with every wind of doctrine, by the sleight of men, and cunning craftiness, whereby they lie in wait to deceive; but speaking the truth in love, may grow up into Him in all things, which is the Head, even Christ; from whom the whole body fitly joined together and compacted by that which every joint supplieth, according to the effectual working in the measure of every part, maketh increase of the body unto the edifying of itself in love." Ephesians 4:8-16. [99]

Apply this rule to the prophetic gift that has been connected with the third angel's message from its rise, and what is the result?—We find that the continual instruction given through Mrs. White has been in the line of unity and harmony, admonishing to "counsel together" and "press together," to be in union with Christ, thus insuring true fellowship and union with one another.

One of the fruits of true gifts mentioned in the letter to the Ephesian church is the gathering of a people into the "unity of the faith." What has been the result in this respect in the rise of the third angel's message?—Fifty-three years ago, when our publications and work were all in the English language, when reference was made to the unity and harmony taught in the testimonies and existing among the believers, our opponents said, "That is very well now, while your work is all in a limited territory, and the believers of one nationality; but should your work spread into different parts of the earth, and gather people of different languages, with their national peculiarities, you would see the *unity* disappear, and your work go to pieces."

Do we see it going to pieces? How is it? The message is now printed, believed, and advocated in sixty-seven languages of the world, and has gained a foothold at different places around the world twice-both north and south of the equator—yet there is the same unity and harmony among those accepting the Lord's counsel through the testimonies [100] as in earlier times. So the visions stand the test of rule seven.

In conclusion, let it be borne in mind that attention has been called in this book to *nine* points of similarity between Mrs. White's visions and those described in the Bible; to *six* points of comparison in the practical work of true vision; and, lastly to *seven* rules. In all of these twenty-two points we find her visions in exact harmony with *true* prophets.

One of the best proofs of the truthfulness of the visions is in the visions themselves. Many of those who read Mrs. White's writings, who know not the origin of the ideas which she advances, say, "When I read Mrs. White's articles it seems to me as though her writings are inspired."

In view of the facts presented in the foregoing pages, it is well for all to heed the admonition of King Jehoshaphat to the host of Judah, "Believe in the Lord your God, so shall ye be established; believe His prophets, so shall ye prosper." 2 Chronicles 20:20.

Adventist Pioneer Library

For more information, visit:

www.APLib.org

or write to:

contact@aplib.org

Made in the USA
Monee, IL
27 June 2023

37658104R00046